EXERCISES IN ARCHITECTURE
learning to think as an architect

Architecture is a doing word. You can learn a great deal about the workings of architecture through analysing examples but a fuller understanding of its powers and potential comes through practice, by trying to do it. As you learn a language you need to practise using it; and as you practise you learn more about what you can do with the language. It is the same with architecture…

This book offers student architects a series of twelve exercises that will develop their capacity for doing architecture. Each exercise is divided into a short series of tasks aimed at developing a particular theme or area of architectural capacity, providing prompts for practice. The exercises deal with themes such as place-making, learning through drawing, framing, light, uses of geometry, stage-setting, the genetics of detail and many more.

Exercises in Architecture builds on and supplements the methodology for architectural analysis presented in the author's previous book *Analysing Architecture* (third edition, Routledge, 2009) and demonstrated in his *Twenty Buildings Every Architect Should Understand* (Routledge, 2010). Together, the three books deal with the three aspects of acquiring any creative discipline: *Analysing Architecture* provides a methodology for analysis that develops an understanding of the way architecture works; *Twenty Buildings* explores and extends that methodology through analysis of examples as case studies; and *Exercises in Architecture* offers a way of expanding understanding and developing capability in architecture by following rudimentary exercises.

Simon Unwin has helped students learn to think as architects for over three decades. He is Emeritus Professor of Architecture at the University of Dundee, Scotland. Previously he taught architectural design and analysis at the Welsh School of Architecture in Cardiff University. He has lived in the UK and Australia, and taught or lectured on his work in China, Israel, India, Sweden, Turkey, Canada and the United States as well as at other schools in the UK and Europe. Simon Unwin's books are used in schools of architecture around the world. *Analysing Architecture* has been translated into Persian, Chinese, Japanese, Spanish and Korean and is currently being translated into Portuguese, Russian and Arabic. He continues to teach at the Welsh School of Architecture in Cardiff.

Some reviews of Simon Unwin's previous book, ***Analysing Architecture***:

'What is striking about the book is the thoughtfulness and consideration which is present in each phrase, each sentence, each plan, each section and each view, all contributing to an overarching quality which makes the book particularly applicable and appropriate to students in their efforts to make sense of the complex and diverse aspects of architecture… Unwin writes with an architect's sensibility and draws with an accomplished architect's hand.'
Susan Rice, Rice and Ewald Architects, *Architectural Science Review*

'Unwin chooses to look at the underlying elements of architecture rather than, as is more usual, at the famous names, styles, movements and chronology of the genre. This rejection of the conventional art-historical approach can lead to interesting conclusions… it is all presented cogently and convincingly through the medium of Unwin's own drawings.'
Hugh Pearman, *The Sunday Times*

'This is an excellent book, recommended to anyone seriously interested in architecture. Its starting point is Unwin's ability to draw well – to think through his hands, as it were. This is fundamental to architectural skill and Unwin has used it to "talk back to himself" and describe the architecture around him. He uses this skill to romp through a huge number and variety of buildings and architectural situations in order to describe architectural strategies. Unwin has at the heart of his book a definition and understanding of architecture that we thoroughly endorse: to be dealt with in terms of its conceptual organisation and intellectual structure. But he adds to this potentially dry definition an emotive overlay or parallel: architecture as the identification of place ("Place is to architecture as meaning is to language"). Thus he takes on the issue of why we value architecture.'
www.architecturelink.org.uk/GMoreSerious2.html

'In clear, precise diagrams and thoughtful text, author Simon Unwin offers an engaging methodology for the study of architecture and aesthetic systems. Time-tested buildings from classical temples to traditional Japanese homes and early modernist masterpieces, are explored in this wide ranging, but focused study. Unwin demonstrates that while architectural styles change over time, the underlying principles that organize quality designs remain remarkably consistent. This book is a must for all architectural students interested in acquiring the visual skills needed to understand a wide variety of design methodologies.'
Diane78 (New York), *Amazon.com website*

'The text has been carefully written to avoid the use of jargon and it introduces architectural ideas in a straightforward fashion. This, I suspect, will give it a well-deserved market beyond that of architects and architectural students.'
Barry Russell, *Environments BY DESIGN*

'From the campsites of primitive man to the sophisticated structures of the late twentieth century, architecture as an essential function of human activity is explained clearly, and illustrated with the author's own excellent drawings. Highly recommended as a well-organized and readable introduction.'
medals@win-95.com, *Amazon.com website*

'This book establishes a systematic method in analyzing architecture. It explains how architectural elements are combined together to form designs that could relate an appropriate sense of "place" specific to the programme as well as the environment surrounding it. The book is well illustrated with diagrams and examples. An extremely useful introductory guide for those who want to learn more about the basics of architecture.'
nikana99@hotmail.com, *Amazon.com website*

Architecture Notebooks *by Simon Unwin:*

The companion website for *Analysing Architecture* may be found at:
www.routledge.com/textbooks/9780415489287/

EXERCISES IN ARCHITECTURE
learning to think as an architect

Simon Unwin

Routledge
Taylor & Francis Group

London and New York

First published 2012
by Routledge
2 Park Square, Milton Park, Abingdon, Oxon OX14 4RN

Simultaneously published in the USA and Canada
by Routledge
711 Third Avenue, New York, NY 10017

Routledge is an imprint of the Taylor & Francis Group, an informa business

British Library Cataloguing in Publication Data
A catalogue record for this book is available from the British Library

Library of Congress Cataloging in Publication Data
Unwin, Simon, 1952-
Exercises in architecture : learning to think as an architect / Simon Unwin.
p. cm.
Includes index.
1. Architecture–Study and teaching. 2. Architecture–Problems, exercises, etc. 3. Architects–Training of.
I. Title. II. Title: Learning to think as an architect.
NA2005.U59 2012
720.76–dc23
2011029785

ISBN: 978-0-415-61908-0 (hbk)
ISBN: 978-0-415-61909-7 (pbk)
ISBN: 978-0-203-13624-9 (ebk)

Designed and typeset in Adobe Garamond Pro and Courier Std by Simon Unwin.

Publisher's note
This book has been prepared from camera-ready copy provided by the author.
Printed by Ashford Colour Press Ltd., Gosport, Hampshire.

MIX
Paper from
responsible sources
FSC® C011748
www.fsc.org

for

Merve and Евгения
(the '*eltis*')

'Instruct them how the mind of man becomes
A thousand times more beautiful than the earth
On which he dwells.'

William Wordsworth – *The Prelude*, 1805

CONTENTS

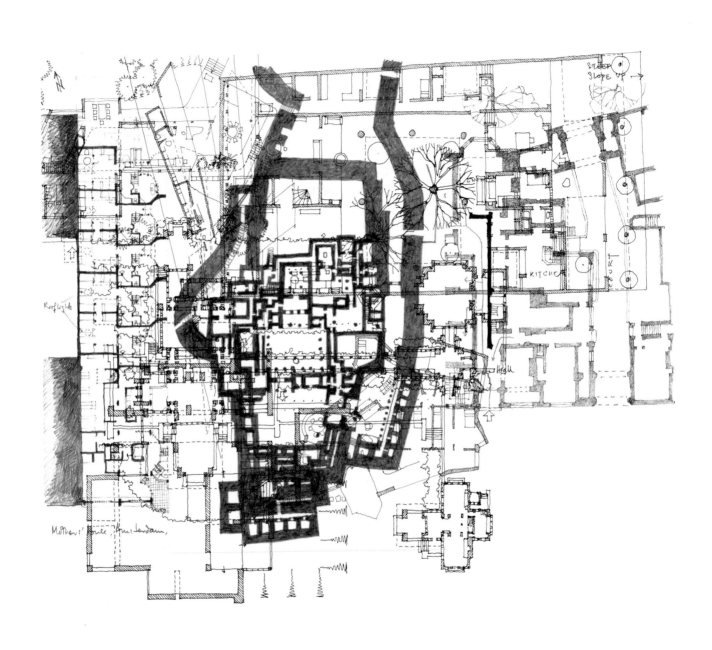

STEEP SLOPE UP

KITCHE

COURT

Hall

Roof Lights

Mothers' Huise Amsterdam,

EXERCISES IN ARCHITECTURE
learning to think as an architect

PRELUDE: the 'architecture' drive

section

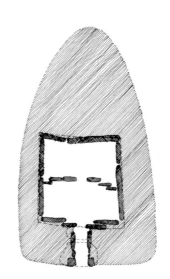

plan

To develop as an architect you need to become aware of the powers of architectural elements: the power of a levelled area of ground to establish a place for a ceremony or performance; the power of a wall to separate one place from another; the power of a roof to shelter or shade; the power of a doorway to allow access...

You have probably taken such architectural elements and their powers for granted since you were born. They are part of the everyday world. But they are an architect's tools.

We grow up surrounded by products of architecture - rooms, gardens, shops, schools, cities... They frame our lives but we treat them as part of the given world. We accept without thought that a wall stops us moving from one location to another while an open doorway lets us through. We know that our home protects us physically and psychologically but do not think consciously about how.

As an architect you need to push through this barrier of familiarity and unthinking acceptance, to become aware of the powers of walls and windows, doorways and roofs, floors and thresholds. You need to become aware of how you can use them to set the spatial matrix within which people go about their lives.

The powers of architectural elements are primitive. Animals use them. Human beings probably used them before we developed verbal language. In a way they constitute their own kind of 'language', the language of space. This language has no words but it is a form of communication. It tells about how spaces accommodate different activities; it tells about who owns which spaces; it tells about boundaries and relationships; it tells about the spatial rules for doing things. Architecture, like poetry, can even elicit emotional responses: excitement, fear, amusement, alienation, trepidation, embarrassment, adoration, privilege... Architecture can transform how you behave, who you think you are, and how you relate to others.

Take this example. The drawings show a dolmen in the Loire region of France. It was built around five and a half thousand years ago. The dolmen is called La Bajoulière and made of very large and very heavy flat slabs of rock.

What was gained by the enormous amount of effort invested in its construction? La Bajoulière was covered in a mound of earth, so what was gained was not a beautiful ornament in the landscape. What its construction did was to create a dark and mysterious interior, separated from everywhere else - an antidote to the daunting uncertainties of the world. It was secure enough to keep out marauding animals and to contain restive spirits and jealous gods.

The architect of La Bajoulière, and those who built it, made a place (in their case an artificial cave) that had not existed before. This is the 'architecture' drive: the drive to amend the world, to rearrange bits of it to establish places to accommodate life (and the dead).

GENERAL INTRODUCTION

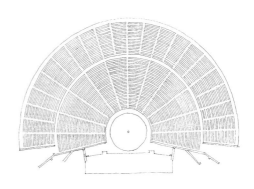

Through architecture the mind sets the spatial matrix for the things we do. By giving form to the theatre, architects in ancient Greece established a place for performance, and relationships between actors, audience, landscape and the gods.

It can be difficult beginning to learn to do architecture. You will have a notion of what architecture is - the design of buildings - but when you start trying to do it the ground disappears from under you. Doing architecture is different, fundamentally different, from (probably) anything you have consciously done before. I say 'consciously' because one of the ways to get a grip on doing architecture is to acknowledge and awaken the architect that you already are: the architect that used to make dens under tables and houses up trees, that still sometimes huddles around a campfire or sits on the lip of a precipice. The following exercises will help by giving you some ground to stand on, literally as well as metaphorically.

'Architecting'

You are an architect but you want to explore what that means. You would like to get better at architecture so you need to practise. This book gives you some exercises that will help you understand what it means to be an architect, how to begin to think architecturally and develop your skills and fluency in this grand and subtle art.

The first step is to realise that architecture is a doing word. Non-architects may tend to treat buildings as products of providence rather than of minds with ideas. The media present buildings as objects to be looked at, enjoyed or criticised (usually the latter). But you have to think of architecture differently - as something you *do* rather than just use or look at. There are buildings or even cities of the future that will never come into existence without you thinking of them first. There are gaps in the built fabric of the world waiting to be filled by your imagination. You are not just a spectator of architecture, you are a player.

Even though architecture is one of the most fundamental things we human beings do in making the world in which we live, it is represented in English only as a noun. 'To design', 'to draw', 'to build' do not adequately convey what it means, if there were such a verb, 'to architect'.

Incidentally, or perhaps significantly, the ancient Greeks did have a verb for doing architecture - ἀρχιτεκτονέω. It means 'to give form to...', as in: *to give form*

3

EXERCISES IN ARCHITECTURE

The essence of architecture consists in giving form to a portion of the world, establishing it as a place and managing spatial relationships.

Example: a girl 'architects' her world

It is a sunny day in early autumn. A young girl (we could call her Eve) has decided to sell apples from the tree in her family's garden. She places a barrow of apples just outside her gate and sits at a table nearby waiting for passers-by. This is an example of the 'architect' in everyone. Eve's small composition of elements has more subtleties than one might at first think. It is positioned adjacent to, but not obstructing, the gateway, where she can withdraw easily into (the safety of) her family territory (defined by the garden hedge) for more apples or for a drink, and where her parents can watch to see she is all right (out there, in the threatening world). As well as the barrow of apples, the girl has a small chair and table with a box of plastic carrier bags and a beaker for money. She has arranged these minimal elements straddling the walkway, to punctuate rather than block the progress of a passer-by. Her back is protected by the hedge. She is shaded by a tree in the grass verge along the roadway... Gateways (thresholds) are always places of transaction, where we meet visitors and say farewell. Building on this, and using other things that are already there, Eve has established ('architected', given form to) a rudimentary shop (for selling apples). For a short time, she has changed the world (a tiny part of it) and her self (into an architect and a shop keeper). This is the power of architecture.

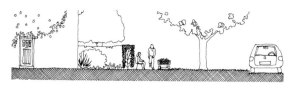

section

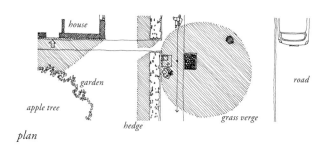

plan

Architecture is, of course, concerned with many other things too - especially the construction of buildings (walls, roofs etc.) and the aesthetic and symbolic appearance of the results... neither of which are minor concerns - but it begins with giving form to places for occupation and use. And 'giving' in this sense includes both recognising the possibilities of things that are there (in this example the pavement, hedge, gate, tree...) as well as amending and adding to them (with the barrow, table, chair...). Eventually (if the planning authorities allowed) Eve might want to add a roof and walls... to make a permanent shop. Then she would worry about how to build it and how it would look.

to a house with its places to cook, eat and sleep; *to give form to* a theatre by drawing a circle on the ground surrounded by seats for spectators; *to give form to* a city by laying out streets, squares and walls; *to give form to* the temple of a god...

We could (and do) use the verb 'to design' for all these, but somehow 'to architect' evokes something more profound, a more primal relationship with the world, in which a mind enters into a proactive relationship with its surroundings and makes sense of (*gives form to*) them by organising (recognising, choosing, arranging, structuring, constructing, composing, moulding, even excavating...)

them into places for occupation and use. In this sense architecture is not merely the art concerned with the cosmetic appearance of buildings, nor only the technology concerned with their construction; it is fundamental to existence. We cannot live in the world without occupying and at least trying to make sense of it in terms of the places in which we do things. Architecture is philosophical (without words); it is the medium through which we set the spatial matrix for just about everything we do. Understood in this way, the challenges and responsibilities of being an architect are fascinating but daunting.

Everyone 'architects' their world – the physical (and philosophical) setting in which they live – at some level, even if it is only setting up a temporary camp or arranging furniture in a room. The present book (together with its sister volume *Analysing Architecture*) addresses how your innate capacity for 'architecting' can be developed to more sophisticated levels where you might feel equipped and confident not only to architect your own world but to offer (professionally) to architect those of others too.

Studying the architectural mind at work

As a mind wishing and willing to take on the challenges and responsibilities of 'architecting' worlds for other people, you must become a student of the ways in which the minds of fellow architects work too. We can learn a great deal about the workings and powers of architecture through analysing examples (as in the present book's other sister volume *Twenty Buildings Every Architect Should Understand*). But, since architecture is a doing word, an operational understanding of its workings and powers can only be acquired through practice, by trying to do it over and over again. We cannot learn language, to ride a bicycle or play the violin, merely by reading how to do it or even by following diagrammatic instructions; we have to

practise – babbling, wobbling, scratching and scraping – before we can become fluent or proficient. It is the same with architecture: the more you practise, the more adept at it your brain becomes and the more you discover what you can do with it. It is with this in mind that the present book offers some exercises for awakening and developing your (already present, innate, latent, dormant) capacity for doing architecture.

The following exercises are intended to help you to practise and develop your ability to think and act as an architect. They are the equivalent of the sorts of exercises you would have been set to develop your ability to use language and mathematics or might have been set to help you learn to think musically as a composer. Language, mathematics, music and architecture, are different modes of thought and creativity but at the same time they are mutually analogous. They are all media through which we make sense of the world. They are all media which require intellectual practice to attain fluency and proficiency. Language works with words and concepts; mathematics with number, measurement and calculation; music with structured sounds, time and emotions. Architecture works with the ground, space, light... by digging and building.

Though sometimes people combine these different media, each occupies its own

5

intellectual realm, requires the brain to
work in its own way, and therefore requires
practice on its own terms. You cannot, for
example, learn to do architecture through
writing words, any more than you could
learn to do mathematics by playing the
flute. The dimensions of practice must be
those of the medium you want to acquire.

Generally in schools of architecture the
norm is to set projects in which students
are asked to design a particular building
type, a work of architecture according to
a specified brief (program): that of a
school, a theatre, a museum, a house or
whatever. This reflects the situation in
the 'real world', where architects are
usually commissioned to design buildings
with a predetermined identity and brief.
It also reflects a long-standing belief
that architecture derives, primarily, from
function. But architecture consists in more
than identity and function. It is a rich
and varied 'language' that has dimensions
beyond pragmatics. The exercises in the
present book are intended to bring out some
of the rich dimensions of architecture.
They do not ignore the dimensions of
function and identity but neither do they
present challenges merely in the form of
asking you to design a particular building
type. The exercises in this book might
best be considered as limbering: exercises
that you can do in preparation for or in
parallel with more orthodox projects.

The following exercises are based on an
understanding: that architecture is, at
origin, a human art concerned with human
life, its experiences and accoutrements;
that human beings are not merely spectators
of architectural 'performances' but vital
ingredients – propagators, modifiers, users
and participants.

The exercises here are not intended
to persuade you to design in any one
particular way but to help you become
aware, through exploration and experiment,
of the varied dimensions of architecture.
Each will take as much time as you can
give it. Some will take no more than a few
moments; others should take more than a day
to complete. Great benefit will be derived
from repeating exercises, discovering new
subtleties each time. The exercises should
help you make thinking as an architect a
habit of mind.

There are no right answers in
architecture (though it is arguable that
there are many 'wrong' ones). As I have
already said, doing architecture is
not like doing sums. You could repeat
each exercise over and over and produce
different but equally good answers each
time. This is something you should
do. To be an architect you cannot be
reticent about being creative; you have
to enjoy doing things. The exercises
are opportunities. If you think of them
as chores then perhaps you should be

devoting your time to a different subject. Architecture is a subtle and difficult art. It needs dedication and involves pain. Being able 'to architect' is not a capacity that can be developed to sophisticated levels quickly and easily.

Drawing (and its limitations)

Drawing is essential to an architect. You cannot be an architect without being able to draw, even if acquiring that skill is a struggle and you are resistant to practising. Drawing, however, is an abstraction; whether on paper or a computer screen, drawing reduces many dimensions to two. This can be problematic when trying to learn to do architecture which fundamentally works in three dimensions (four if you include time). For this reason, the exercises in this book ask you to work with real materials, either children's building blocks and a bread board, or found materials in the landscape.

Learning to do architecture involves a particular kind of learning. It is not a matter of learning a particular body of knowledge - as one might in learning the facts of history - nor is it about learning a particular method to follow to produce a predictable outcome - as one might in following a recipe to produce a specific dish, or a formula to produce a particular calculation. Learning to do architecture is more like learning language than anything else - allowing one's mind (intellect and imagination) gradually to experience what it is able to do with a particular medium. So try not to get frustrated when it is not easy. Learning to do architecture is not a matter of following instructions. Even though it would be possible to offer instructions to produce particular kinds of architecture, such a method would diminish the contribution your own imagination might make.

Small children first learn language as an instrument, they use it to do things: to get more food; to ask someone to open the door; to have teddy returned to them from the floor... Think of architecture in the same way. Think what you can use a wall, a doorway, a window, a roof... to *do*. Consider this before you wonder what it should be made of or will look like.

The Exercises

The following exercises are divided into three sections: 'Fundamentals', 'Geometry' and 'Out into the Real World'. Each section contains a number of exercises, each of which is divided into a series of tasks. There are twelve exercises in all but some fifty-eight component tasks.

The 'Fundamentals' section deals with the basic drive of architecture to establish (identify) place.

The 'Geometry' section deals with the various kinds of architectural geometry, as discussed in the 'Geometries of Being' and 'Ideal Geometry' chapters in *Analysing Architecture* (Routledge, 2009).

The 'Out into the Real World' section asks you to take the lessons you have learnt in the first two sections and apply them in real situations by making (temporary) places in the landscape.

Interludes and Observations

Interspersed amongst the exercises you will also find some 'Interludes' and 'Observations', short extra chapters that illustrate and discuss in detail some general issues that arise from the exercises. The Interludes add breadth and depth to the themes covered by analysing specific examples. The Observations introduce some theoretical issues pertinent to their related exercises.

You will already have seen the 'Prelude' at the beginning of the book. At the end is a short 'Postlude' on drawing.

Materials and equipment

Any materials and equipment needed for each exercise are listed where appropriate. The exercises in 'Fundamentals' and 'Geometry' sections are conducted using simple building blocks and a flat board. Those in

the 'Out into the Real World' section are to be conducted using real materials in real locations in the landscape you have to hand.

Keeping a notebook

You will also need a good notebook – as described in *Analysing Architecture* – in which to catch ideas, record and reflect on designs, experiment with draft designs, and to store information from a mixture of sources that might be relevant to your work. Keeping a notebook is a serious and enjoyable activity. You will find your own way of doing it. But, initially at least, it does require commitment. Keeping a notebook is essential to becoming an architect. We learn to do things not so much by being told or shown how to do them (though both listening and watching play their part) but most effectively by engaging our own minds and bodies with the medium in which we want to work and discovering for ourselves what we can do with it. Very young children do this with language. In their minds they collect words and ideas, and put them together in their attempts to talk. Gradually their language becomes more and more sophisticated.

You need to do something similar to learn the 'language' of architecture. Like the child with ideas and words, you should collect architectural ideas and

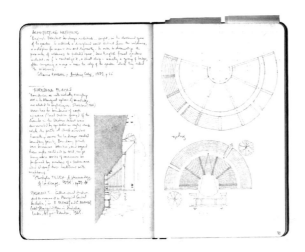

You can download some of my notebooks at simonunwin.com.

the forms by which they are manifest and experiment with them in your own work. But (unlike the child and language) you cannot do this just in your mind. Architecture depends on physical manifestation or representation. You need an appropriate 'arena' in which to engage with it. It is impossible to build every architectural idea you encounter or have but you can usually draw them. A plain notebook is a good arena in which to collect and experiment with architectural ideas and forms. Engaging with architecture in this way, you will increase your appreciation of its powers and possibilities. Keeping a notebook should become a habit you continue throughout your career.

Through the present book, you will be prompted to follow up and underpin the exercises by collecting pertinent examples in your notebook and experimenting with the ideas introduced.

Producing good work

The American poet Alfred Joyce Kilmer (1886-1918) wrote 'I think that I shall never see a poem lovely as a tree'. Though he did not deny outright the possibility that someone, perhaps he, might write 'a poem lovely as a tree', this line may be interpreted as suggesting that it is unlikely that human creativity could ever match the beauty of nature. Leaving aside the sophistry for the mind that it itself could be said to be a part of nature, and hence that poems are themselves natural creations(!), that suggestion, for an architect, should be resisted.

You can enjoy a film, or a piece of music, or a detective story... But when you think about it, you find that what you are really enjoying is the creative capacity of another human mind. You take vicarious pleasure in seeing what a fellow mind can do. You can be entertained by the ingenious way in which Sherlock Holmes (or Inspector Morse) solves a case but at the same time (and perhaps subliminally) you appreciate more Arthur Conan Doyle's (or Colin Dexter's) achievement in concocting the story. You can laugh at Jeeves and Bertie Wooster (or the occupants of *The Office*) but it is the author P.G. Wodehouse (or Ricky Gervais) that deserves the major portion of the applause. You can be enraptured by the sensuality of a trio from the opera *Cosi Fan Tutte* but you are also admiring the subtlety and wit of Mozart's composition. You can be captivated by the imagery in the film *Nostalghia* but you are also impressed by Tarkovsky's imagination and direction.

The aesthetic appreciation of creative work veils a profound celebration of the perception, intelligence, imagination, judgement, inventiveness, ingenuity, intellectual skill of the human mind. The same is equally true of appreciating a finely honed philosophical argument, a clever and productive scientific experiment, an economical and efficient computer program, a ruthless and elegant strategy in chess... and of course a beautifully, poetically, inventively conceived work of architecture.

Concoction, composition, direction, invention, ingenuity, strategy are all synonyms for architecture. These constitute the challenges that face you. You are asked to produce architectural poems more lovely than trees. And that means celebrating and taking joy in the creative capacity of your own mind.

Taking joy in the creative capacity of your mind is not a passive activity. It means filling your imagination with what others have done. It means being prolific and generous with ideas. It means understanding the cultural and physical conditions within which you are working. It means rigour in thinking things through. It means care and consideration in presenting your ideas to others. It means self-critical reflection and a willingness to redo work over and over again until you feel it is right.

There is no method for producing great architecture. All these exercises can do is lead you into areas where you might begin to realise how architecture works and discover some of its limitless potential. Greatness is up to you but understanding what is possible might help.

This book of exercises should be read in conjunction with other books in the series – *Analysing Architecture*; *An Architecture Notebook*; *Doorway*; *Twenty Buildings Every Architect Should Understand* (all published by Routledge) – as well as many others, some of which are included in the recommended Reading list at the end of this book.

There is more to architecture than can be encompassed in the following few exercises. I hope however they will help you at least begin to think as an architect.

Simon Unwin, September 2011

Section One

FUNDAMENTALS

FUNDAMENTALS

These first exercises explore the fundamentals of architecture. They will involve you in doing things, so you will need to be prepared to find that old set of building blocks you played with when you were small. You will also need your notebook and a sharp pencil.

Architecture originates in the mind but its products are (or at least they are intended to be) real. An architect's intention is to build real buildings, with real materials, in real conditions, to accommodate real people. To begin to develop your capacity for architecture it is necessary to experience it, as far as possible, as a physical as well as intellectual activity. To some extent this can be done by building models but it also means going outside – to the beach or into the woods – collecting and assembling stuff, and making real places. (You will be asked to do this in the final set of exercises in this book.)

Even so, because of the expensive and time-consuming nature of building, it rapidly becomes impractical to build all your ideas in reality. You will need to become proficient as an architect before anyone will be willing to spend good money on making your ideas into real buildings. So you must learn to do architecture in abstract. You will have to understand the relationship between reality, including the imagined reality of your architectural

ideas, and its representation in models and drawing. This involves intellectual as well as manual practice.

These then are the two aims of this first set of exercises: to explore the fundamentals of architecture through playing with real materials – your blocks – and to learn about what it is that we give form to with architecture.

Growing up and being human involves recognising and giving form to lots of things and learning how to do so. We live by form. The first form we encounter is probably our mother's face with its orderly arrangement of eyes, nose and mouth. Soon after we learn that sound can be given form as a tune or lullaby, with its orderly arrangement of notes in rhythm. Our days follow a pattern of sleeping and being awake which gradually comes to match that of night and day. Slowly we realise that thoughts can be given form in language, through words and sentences. We might learn to draw, first scribbling but then acquiring the skill of making marks to look like a cat, a house, our mother's face... Eventually we learn to write, giving visible form to our language with an alphabet of letters and vocabulary of words. The 'substance' being given form in each of these cases is very different. In a tune it is the sound of a voice; the substance given form in language is thought expressed as sound shaped into words and

sentences; that of drawing, visual shape represented in two dimensional marks on paper.

There are many other examples that stretch into adult life. We give form to quantity with number and learn the rules of mathematics. Visual shape can be represented not only in two dimensions by drawing and painting but also three dimensionally in sculpture, by moulding clay and carving wood or stone. Movement is given form in dance and gymnastics. Passing time is given form by clocks and calendars. By following recipes we give form to our food. By knitting a jumper we give form to wool. We make each other laugh in the form of jokes. Maps give form to the layout of cities and land. We give form to our understanding of the workings of nature through science. Journalists give form to chaotic events by turning them into news stories. Morality is given form through religion and philosophy, and set down as laws. Social relationships are given form through friendship and the structure of organisations. We even attempt to give conflict form by the rules of games or military strategy.

This list is far from complete; life involves giving form to all sorts of things. We make sense of our world by giving it form. But what is it that we give form to with architecture? The answer might seem obvious: buildings. But the following exercises will show that it is not quite that simple. Architecture has many substances.

Materials

You will need your set of children's building blocks, preferably not ones that clip together. You could do some of the following exercises using clip together blocks (such as Lego) but, since they impose strict geometric rules and can be stuck together in ways that defy gravity, you will have more flexibility and gain a more realistic sense of structure if you use simple wooden blocks. (These also have their geometric predisposition – though not so rigid – but we shall talk about that later.) For the ground on which to build you will need a flat board – a large bread board or small drawing board will do.

You will also need a small person, the smallest artist's manikin you can find; (two or three will be better).

Do not worry that these exercises might seem a childish start to learning to do architecture; there is a lot you can learn about the substances and workings of architecture using such simple materials. The small person, however, is essential.

EXERCISE 1: the substance without substance

In this exercise you will begin to explore the activities of giving form and making place, which lie at the heart of all architecture. The exercise introduces the two fundamental substances of architecture: material and space. You will be familiar with giving form to material – clay, cardboard, building blocks... – but the suggestion that you can give form to space might seem a little strange.

We tend to understand the world as a collection of objects, physical things that we can see and possibly touch: a book; a tree; a motor car; a leaf; a sweater; an ocean; a sandwich... Such objects consist of physical material: paper, wood, metal, cellulose, wool, water, bread, cheese... Buildings are made of physical materials: stone, brick, glass, concrete, timber, titanium, copper... and we can see them

too as objects. But the first (and trickiest) thing to understand about architecture is that in it we give form to space as well as to physical material.

The activity of giving form is intellectual and physical. Put simply: you have an idea about what you want to make; you choose your material; and you impose your idea onto it. For example: you have an idea of making a model of a horse; you choose clay; you mould the clay into the form of a horse. But how can you impose an idea onto space, which has no substance?

This first exercise will help you begin to understand spatial ideas and how space can be given form. It will also take you a significant step further. It will demonstrate how you give space the architectural equivalent of meaning; how you make a 'place'.

EXERCISE 1a. Imposing an idea.

Find your building blocks and a rectangular board – 300mm (12″) by 450mm (18″) will be adequate. Begin by playing as you would have done when you were a child. Empty the blocks onto the board.

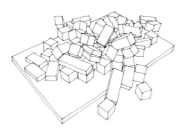

Your pile of blocks has no form other than that produced by the way they have fallen. Now do the first thing every child is encouraged to do by a parent: build a tower as high as you can.

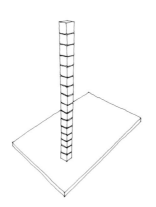

This is your first architectural idea. It may not be original but it is nevertheless powerful. The tower could never have built itself. Neither chance nor any of the mindless processes according to which the universe operates could have produced it.

The tower is a manifestation of the ability of your mind to give form: to have an idea and, by the dexterity of your hand, to impose that idea on to physical material – in this case, your building blocks.

Even though this activity is commonplace, it is still astonishing. When you were small you were possibly so affected by the power manifest in your tower – your ability to assert your will over matter – that you knocked it over, laughing excitedly; returning the blocks to a state of formlessness. (And if another child built a tower, you might have been mean enough to demolish that too.)

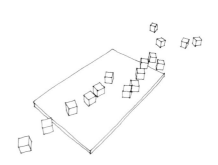

EXERCISE 1b. Centre.

You built your tower as a material object
but it stood in *space*, the space defined
by your board. You can begin to understand
space as a substance of architecture by
thinking about the power of putting an
object in a specific location.

You probably built your tower somewhere
near the centre of your board though
perhaps without plotting its location
exactly. Now measure the exact centre of
your board (the easiest way is by drawing
diagonals) and rebuild your tower there.

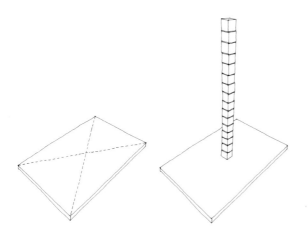

Your tower has now acquired a special,
more powerful, presence. The centre is a
privileged location; there is only one of
them, as against any number of locations
that are NOT the centre. The centre of a
space possesses its own authority.

EXERCISE 1c. Identification of place (by object).

You have built your tower in the
artificial setting of a rectangular board
with a measurable centre. Now imagine
your tower as an obelisk in featureless
open countryside. (Imagining ideas in
real settings is essential to doing
architecture.) In this situation, without a
definite measurable centre to occupy, your
tower establishes its own.

Your tower gives the landscape a centre
it did not previously have. It marks
a place, a specific location amid the
featureless surroundings. It establishes a
point of reference in relation to which you
would know where you were.

Stop imagining. Return your attention to
the tower in the centre of your board.

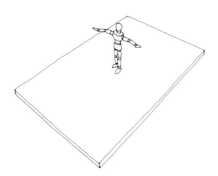

EXERCISE 1d. Introducing the person.

Next, find your small person - a small artists' manikin will be perfect. Stand it on the board, looking at the tower. You are not doing this to add scale (though it does that too) but to model the relationship between the tower and the person.

Empathise with your person. (Empathy too is essential in architecture.) You are looking at this tower that occupies the centre of your world. The tower is the object of your attention.

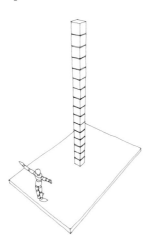

Maybe you are in awe of the tower, subject to its manifestation of power. Maybe you worship it. Maybe you are suspicious of its arrogance and want to challenge its authority by throwing stones at it or demolishing it.

EXERCISE 1e. Person at the centre.

Demolish the tower... Take the object away and put your person (your self) in its place right at the centre of the board.

Now it is the person (you) that occupies the special privileged position.

EXERCISE 1f. Identification of place (by person).

Now, as you did with your tower, imagine yourself out in that featureless open countryside.

You too (like the tower) establish a centre in the landscape. You too identify a place. But you are a living centre; you move; you need room to do things, to live, to dance. You need space.

The person is essential to architected space. The tower you built only *represented* your presence as its perpetrator.

When the Norwegian architect Sverre Fehn wanted to illustrate the idea 'Man and space' (or 'Man and the Room') he did a sketch like this one (left, 1996). You can see the original reproduced in Fjeld - The Pattern of Thoughts, *2009, p. 286.*

EXERCISE 1g. Circle of place.

Using the centre you have already marked on your board, draw a circle as large as possible.

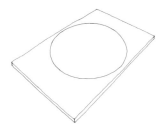

This is your second architectural idea. The circle of place is essential to architecture. It is the antithesis of the tower seen as an object. Even the tower generates a circle of place around it. (See *Analysing Architecture*, 'Geometries of Being'.)

Now stand your person at the centre of the circle.

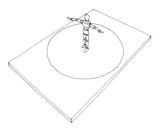

This circle is not just an abstract geometric shape (such as you would have drawn in school geometry lessons). It delimits a space that belongs to the person. The circle identifies a place but not in the same way as the tower. It *frames* space. And the person occupies the frame as a place to be (rather than as a spectator). The circle defines, literally, the *circumstance* of the person. The person is no longer a spectator (as of the tower) but an ingredient, a participant in this rudimentary work of architecture.

In drawing the circle on the ground (the board) you have begun to give form to space - the substance that has no substance. In framing a place, your circle draws a line - a boundary - between a specific inside and everywhere else - the great outside. Framing place is fundamental to architecture. And the frame, whether merely a circle drawn in the sand or the walls of a full scale building, mediates between content - occupants and their activities - and context - the great outside.

The circle on the ground defines a boundary and asserts a claim for possession of space that, in the real world, might have to be defended. Circles of place can be as small as the saucer where your cup of tea rests, or as large as a country. In our homes we each have our circle of place. We make sense of the world in which we live in terms of circles of place.

EXERCISE 1h. Threshold.

As well as establishing a boundary, the line of the circle defines a threshold – an interface where you pass from outside to inside and back again. With its emotional prompt, the threshold is at least as powerful, architecturally, as the centre.

Stand your person just outside the circle, facing in.

Use your imagination again, to role play. Imagine how it feels: to stand at the edge; to cross the line; to enter the circle, to move around inside, and then to stand precisely at its centre. Imagine the difference between: being outside; being inside; and the strangely unresolved state of being in-between, just on the line, neither inside nor out. Architecture deals in these three basic positions.

Do this adopting different personas. Recognise the circle as an instrument of social relationship. Enter the circle first as the person who drew it and claims to be its rightful occupant. Then do it as a welcome visitor to someone else's circle, maybe waiting for permission to enter. Then as a suspect stranger; a trespasser; a thief; an attacker intent on taking the circle for your own... Stand outside the circle as someone who is not allowed to enter, excluded, exiled.

Watch as a privileged person – a priest, a 'noble', a man (or a woman)... who *is* allowed to go inside the circle – crosses the line. Stare at the person who is now isolated from the world by the circle. Imagine yourself as that privileged person being stared at. Be aware of the mix of emotions prompted by your relationship with this simple (simplest possible?) work of architecture. Recognise that drawing a circle on the ground can be a political, and provocative, act; giving form to space for human occupation always is. You are beginning to witness, and see the possibilities of manipulating, some of the powers of architecture.

IN YOUR NOTEBOOK...

**In your notebook... collect circles of
place**. Record them as simple drawings
with notes describing where they are, how
they are defined, what thing or activity
they contain (a circle of place must have
content). Circles of place do not have to
be perfectly circular. They may be tiny or
huge.

Bring to mind circles of place from your
memory: perhaps the circle you drew in
chalk on the pavement to play marbles with
your friends; or the circle you and your
schoolmates made watching a playground
fight.

Become conscious of circles of place
you encounter in your surroundings, while
wandering, and depicted in the media.
Pause to draw each in your notebook.
Draw as much as you can but also note
characteristics that cannot be drawn
easily: the relationship of a circle of
place (an ancient stone circle perhaps)
with a distant feature in the landscape;
variations in the consistency or texture
of the ground (as around a green on a golf
course, which is the circle of place around
the hole with its marker flag).

Consider how circles of place are made
other than by drawing a line on the ground;
by, for example: the canopy of a tree;
temperature (as around a fire); sound (as
around a speaker or musician); smell (as
around curry cooking on the stove or a
particularly malodorous person); light

*We make a circle of place when we sit together
around a camp fire.*

*A candle generates a circle (or sphere) of place
around itself with its light.*

(as around a candle or projected by a spotlight); wi-fi (as around a router).

Be alert for circles of place that are concentric (as in the performance circle – *orkestra* – of an ancient Greek theatre surrounded by the larger circle of tiers on which the audience sat) or that overlap (as when the circle of place of an outdoor cafe overlaps and contains the circles of place of a number of tables, each of which overlaps and contains the circles of place of each of the individual settings).

Be aware of circles of place that have personal meaning to you and those that are of public significance. (Your family will remember where and when your cat was buried whereas a large number of fans will remember where and when England won a cricket match against Australia (e.g. at the Sydney Cricket Ground in January 2011).

There is no time limit to this notebook exercise. You could still be collecting circles of place for decades to come. As an architect it is essential that you can see the world in terms of circles of place and understand how and why they are made. The establishment of circles of place lies at the core of doing architecture.

On June 3, 2011 the Guardian newspaper (UK) published a large photograph of a recent exorcism being performed in Colombia. This drawing shows the layout. The 'possessed' person was 'crucified' on the ground surrounded by a circle of place defined by flowers and a line of ash.

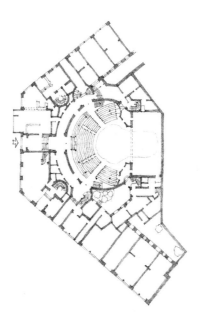

A theatre frames a circle of place for performance. This is the plan of the Bouffes du Nord in Paris, a nineteenth century theatre that was remodelled in the 1980s by director Peter Brook. He changed it from a proscenium arch theatre into one where the audience sits around an arena. (See Andrew Todd and Jean-Guy Lecat – The Open Circle, 2003.)

21

EXERCISE 2: flipping perceptions

Together, the tower and the circle (of Exercise 1) constitute the 'Big Bang' of architecture. They manifest the 'moment' when the mind imposes an idea on (asserts its will over) the world as found. When the mind begins to intervene, the world is changed. The tower and circle identify place in different ways. But together they constitute the reciprocal substances of architecture: matter (physical material) and (occupiable) space.

EXERCISE 2a. Container for a dead person.

One of the oldest types of permanent building is a burial chamber. We can use it in this exercise as a simple example of how material and space work together in architecture.

First, lie your person as a corpse at the centre of the circle you have already drawn on your board (1).

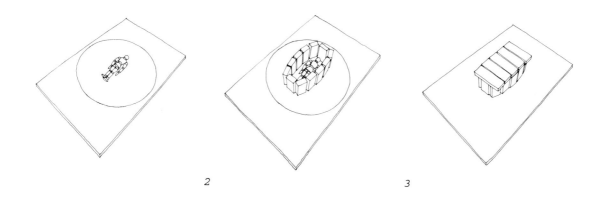

1   2   3

In Exercise 2 we shall see how perception of a work of architecture can flip between the two.

'Draw' a 'circle' in standing 'stones' (blocks) around the body. Your dead friend is not going to need any living space, so draw the circle of stones tight around the body, distorting it as necessary (2). This 'circle' of stones frames the body. Give it a roof of larger stones (3), entombing the body.

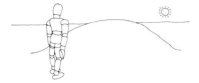

Stand another (living) person on the board, looking at the burial chamber.

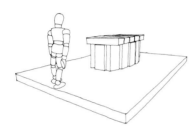

This person sees your construction of stones as an object standing on the ground.

You assembled the stones to give form to space, the substance without substance. Your purpose was to identify an interior place, an enclosed space for occupation, in this case by your dead friend. But the person outside sees the burial chamber as an object; sees it in terms of giving form to physical material. This is a characteristic flip in the perception of works of architecture. You live in your house and do many things in its spaces; but, standing outside or in your imagination, you and others see the house as an object.

Shortly we shall look at giving form to space for the living but for the moment we shall stay with architecture for the dead.

EXERCISE 2b. Pyramid.

Many ancient burial chambers were covered with earth (top), which suggests their architects thought of them less as objects and more as interior spaces like artificial caves within artificial hills. Even so, a mound may be seen in the landscape as an object. And your (the architect's) mind might turn to thinking about how it should look. From the primary intent of giving form to a small space for the containment of a dead body, attention turns to giving appropriate form to the external appearance of the tomb.

You might for example, as the ancient Egyptians did, decide to form your mound in the ideal geometric shape of a four-sided pyramid finished with shaped stone blocks.

23

But the pyramid may be dismantled, back to the chamber at its centre...

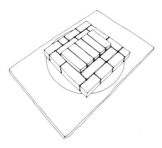

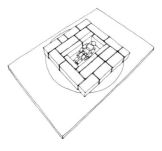

... and to the notional circle around the corpse...

... from which the work of architecture - pyramid and burial chamber - began.

In the pyramid, solid matter has been given an ideal geometric form but its architecture depends on the space for occupation by the corpse at its centre. Notice that, in the form of that space, the distorted circle of the burial chamber has (like the square around the table in Marina Abramovic's 'The Artist is Present, see page 27) become a rectangle. There is a formal resonance between the person, the world and the processes of building, which is manifest in the rectangle. In architecture the circle of place is often transformed into a rectangle. In later exercises, we shall look further at the relationship between the rectangle, the person and the processes of making buildings.

The burial chamber and pyramid were places for the dead. Now we shall begin to explore giving form to space for life.

EXERCISE 2c. Theatre and house.

Begin again with the circle. This time, rather than having a static (dead) person at its centre, populate the circle with people interacting.

The space inside the circle becomes an arena for life open to public view: a performance place – the *orkestra* of an ancient Greek theatre; a place for combat – the *dojo* for sumo wrestling; or perhaps a place for ritual, open debate or the dispensation of justice.

Next, begin to make the circle into a private and sheltered place – a house. We shall assume that your place for life is in a climate that may be wet and cold, so put a hearth at the centre of the circle and sit your people around it being sociable.

The hearth provides a focus for life in the circle; the fire will be useful for cooking as well as keeping you warm. The arena has begun to be an exclusive and comfortable enclave, a home. You can imagine, in darkness, the hemisphere of light and warmth emanating from the fire, with the people sitting inside.

The inhabitants of this rudimentary home are going to need privacy and a bit more space than the corpse, so this time build an enclosing wall at least as large as the circle on your board. The corpse was going to stay put; but your living inhabitants will want to go in and out of their house, so you will need to leave a gap in your wall for a doorway.

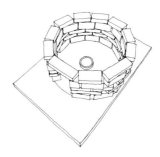

Now think of a simple way of organising the inside to accommodate the inhabitants' activities.

25

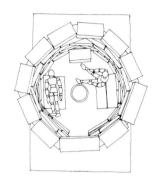

1

Here (1) I have provided two beds either
side of the central hearth and a table for
the inhabitants' possessions. Notice that
each of these creates its own 'circle of
place' within the larger circle of place
enclosed by the walls. Together they
establish a spatial rule system (like the
court or pitch on which a game is played)
that suggests, if not determines, how the
space may be used. These circles of place
relate to each other and interact: there is
'your bed' and 'the other person's bed';
the table is in reach from both the beds.
The fire radiates its warmth over the beds
but is contained by the walls. Notice
too that the doorway establishes its own
threshold/entrance place.

Of course your doorway will have a door,
and the house a roof to shelter it from
the weather. On a circular house, the roof
might be a conical structure of branches
tied together and covered with thatch (2).

2

With its roof on, the house (3), like
the burial chamber, may be seen in two
different ways: an inhabitant sees it as
an interior place, a refuge into which to
withdraw from the world to sleep in warmth
and safety; a person looking from outside
sees it as an object in the landscape and
begins to wonder whether it looks beautiful
or how it might be made to look better (in
whatever way). Architecture deals in both
perceptions, giving form to space and to
the object.

3

INTERLUDE: 'The Artist is Present'

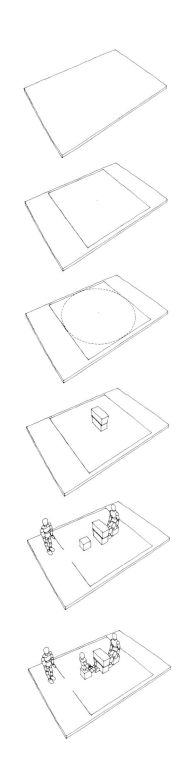

1

2

3

4

5

6

From March to May 2010, the artist Marina Abramovic staged a 'performance' in the Atrium of New York's Museum of Modern Art (MOMA). Entitled 'The Artist is Present', it provides a good illustration of the architectural powers explored in Exercise 1. You will find some photographs of 'The Artist is Present' at: www.moma.org/visit/calendar/exhibitions/965 (November 2010)

Abramovic's equivalent of your board was the floor of the Atrium (1). On this she had inscribed a large square defined by a white line (2). This square identified a place in the same way as your circle (3). At the centre, Abramovic had positioned a table - like an altar - a place of mediation, communion, intercourse (4). A chair was placed either side of the table; she sat on one of them; opposite her was the other chair and a gap in the boundary line, opening a 'doorway' - a threshold - into her 'domain' (5). Visitors were invited to come and sit opposite her, one at a time. Others waited at the threshold (6). Each could sit with her as long as they wanted or could survive her inscrutable (implacable) gaze.

Whatever else this work means, its setting invoked the architectural powers of the boundary, centre and threshold. The square framed the performance, creating a 'sacred' area around the 'altar' (table). Spectators and waiting visitors were kept outside (excluded) by the white line. The table, across which each visitor in turn communed silently with the artist, occupied the centre. The threshold identified the point of entrance, eliciting a frisson for visitors as each stepped over it and approached the table to take the seat opposite Abramovic. The setting itself was framed by bright lights. Abramovic sat impassively at her table during the daily opening hours of MOMA for three months. Many hundreds of visitors came to subject themselves to, or challenge, her gaze. Some wept.

If architecture can be compared to language, then Abramovic's layout may be seen as an architectural equivalent, though slightly more complex because of the 'altar' and doorway, of the sentence 'the cat sat on the mat'.

IN YOUR NOTEBOOK...

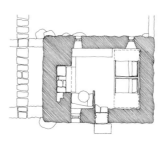

In your notebook... collect examples of perceptions flipping. Find a very small dwelling – a one-roomed building in which someone lives. It might be your own house or one you find in a book. You will however need to be able to tell how the space of the house is used. Do a careful drawing, in plan, of how the space of the house is arranged: draw the furniture, rugs, bedding... as accurately (in size and position) as you can. Note on your drawing how the various areas are or might be used – a place for preparing food, for storing fuel, for sleeping, for washing... Describe in your drawing the life of the space.

Now draw the same dwelling as an object standing on the ground in space (as an elevation or three-dimensional drawing). Again, do the drawing as accurately as you can, being careful about the proportions of the various parts and including any ornamental touches. You could also record the different colours and textures of the different materials used in the building.

Ask yourself which of the two drawings best illustrates the 'architecture' of the building. The answer must be 'both'. But whereas the 'object' drawing represents only external appearance, the plan drawing illustrates the life of the house. Architecture deals in both.

You can do the same exercise with different buildings, maybe a small temple or chapel.

This small cottage in Wales was built as a place to live: a refuge protected from the weather and other people. Within its walls and under its roof it has one room organised into places to cook, to eat, to sleep... all arranged in relation to the entrance, the hearth and the three small windows.

The cottage may be beautiful. It was built without pretension, straightforwardly, with care and understanding of inhabitants' needs and the materials available rather than concern for outward show.

The cottage below, by contrast, was designed with an extra level of concern for its outward appearance. Because of this (some might say) it is more a work of 'architecture'. But (others might respond that) there is architecture in the spatial organisation of the Welsh cottage.

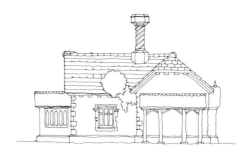

AN OBSERVATION: appearance and experience

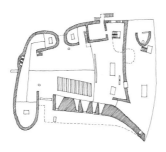

There is architecture in the organisation of space as well as in the composition of external form. To external appearance the person is only a spectator. To spatial organisation the person is the prime ingredient, the player on the stage.

[You should recognise the building above. You should also know who designed it, where it is and when it was built. If you do not know, you will find it in any book on the history of twentieth century architecture.]

Sometimes it might seem as if architecture is primarily concerned with the appearances of buildings, internal as well as external. Certainly the media seem to portray it in this way and the photographs in magazines and architectural history books reinforce this way of seeing architecture. But the aesthetics of a building are not confined to its visual appearance. They involve personal response to the forms of space. A person's experience of space includes emotional responses - to being 'at the centre', 'at the threshold', 'excluded' or 'included'... - as well as the pragmatic use of spaces for particular purposes. The following exercises will show that architecture, in being the medium through which we give form to space as well as to material, has richer and more diverse aspects than visible material form: aspects that influence, or even manage, how we experience space, how we behave and how we relate to each other in various circumstances.

The next exercise, related to the previous ones, introduces one of the most powerful, and much used, spatial devices of architecture - the axis. Though it involves the eye, this device is more to do with relationships than appearances.

EXERCISE 3: axis (and its denial)

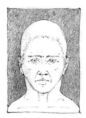

You may have noticed that what you have been doing so far in these exercises has been influenced by different sorts of geometry. We shall review these later. But first we shall add another: the axis. You might have seen it emerge in your block models (and in the setting of Abramovic's 'The Artist is Present'). After the centre and the threshold, the axis is a fundamental architectural device. Though it may be seen in material form - as in the line that runs down the centre of a human body or the front elevation (portico) of a classical temple - the axis, born of alignment of doorway and eye (line of sight), belongs first to space.

The external form of the human body has an axis down its middle: with a foot, leg, testicle, breast, shoulder, arm, hand, nostril, eye, ear... on each side. But its most powerful axis is the one that strikes out from its eyes - the line of sight. This is an axis in space.

EXERCISE 3a. Doorway axis.

The doorway of the house establishes a place of transition between the world outside and the refuge inside. Its threshold faces two ways: inwards and out.

Stand your person outside looking in.

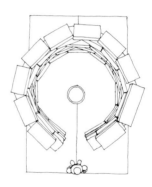

The person's line of sight, passing through the doorway, establishes an axis that links the person with the hearth at the centre of the circle.

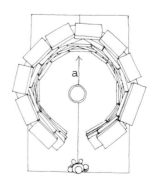

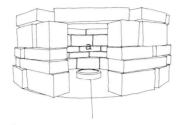

The doorway – a fulcrum between the two – acts like the sight of a rifle. The axis also extends beyond the hearth to hit the wall, identifying a significant position (a) directly opposite the doorway. From the point of view of the person outside, the doorway frames this significant position, as in a picture.

Because of the doorway, the space of the house acquires a more complex form. The doorway, collaborating with the eye of the person, has added an invisible line – the axis – to the circle with its centre. This axis is a line of sight that identifies a second privileged place (in addition to the centre) at or on the wall opposite the doorway.

The doorway and its axis generate a hierarchy of places within the house. There was a similar hierarchy in Abramovic's 'The Artist is Present' (see page 27):

EXERCISE 3b. Quartering.

The axis, in your house and in 'The Artist is Present', is also a line of passage along which the person enters (or aspires to enter) the circle of place. The axis born of the doorway and eye introduces a dynamic line, a line of movement into the innately static – centred – circle or square. In the house (though the hearth is an obstacle) this dynamic line terminates at the wall directly opposite the doorway. In 'The Artist is Present' the dynamic line terminates at Abramovic herself, sitting on her 'throne' at the table, waiting.

The axis plays a third role in the spatial form of the interior of your house. It divides the space into two halves – left and right – suggesting a second axis at right angles to the first.

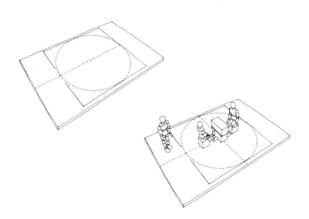

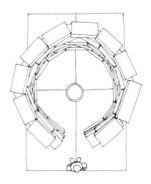

The arrangement of places inside the house is related to these two axes, with a bed at either side and the table at the significant position directly opposite the doorway.

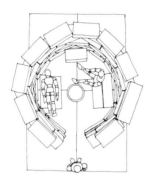

The hearth retains its central position. The two axes, introduced into the circle of the house by the doorway, provide a spatial framework for the organisation of the interior into subsidiary places. The framework of axes lends the organisation of the space an apparent 'rightness' – a spatial harmony perhaps comparable to the harmony of a major chord in music, the syntax of a simple sentence or the balance of a mathematical equation.

EXERCISE 3c. Relating to the remote.

Remove the furniture from the house. Position your person (yourself) at position (a) by the wall looking directly out of the doorway.

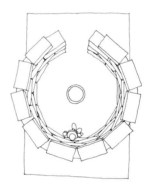

Now the axis works in the opposite direction. It strikes outwards, even beyond the edge of your board (your world), beyond the horizon.

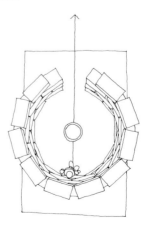

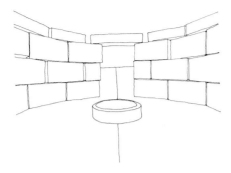

The rectangle of the doorway frames a 'picture' of the world outside with the axis striking out into the distance.

This axis, generated by your eye in conjunction with the doorway, can establish a link between the interior of your house – your person, the hearth... – and something in the distance; an object...

The house with its doorway becomes an instrument of association. It stretches out an invisible 'finger' to touch something seen as important but remote. The frame of the doorway with its axis enhances the importance of the remote. It allows the influence of that remote something to penetrate to the core of the house.

With the axis, the form architecture can give to space stretches beyond the confines of walls, even to infinity.

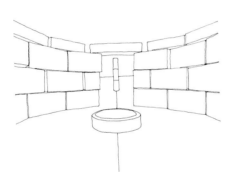

... a mountain or perhaps the sun rising or setting at the horizon.

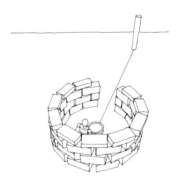

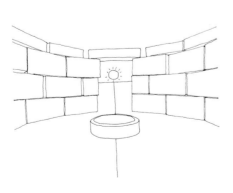

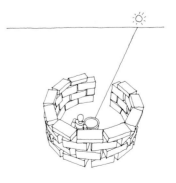

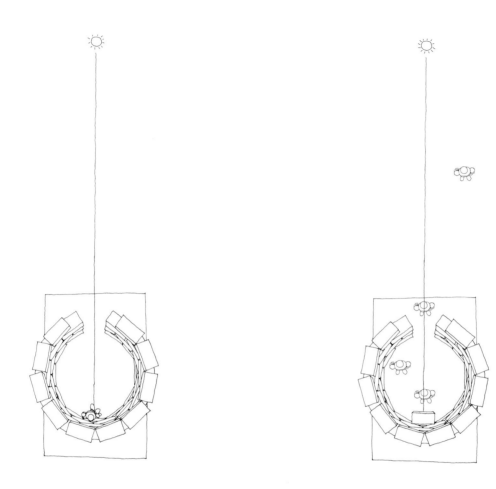

EXERCISE 3d. Temple.

Remove the hearth; see your person as a king or a goddess and you have transformed the house from a domestic refuge into a throne room or a temple. Replace your king or goddess with an altar – a place of mediation, communion, intercourse – attended by a priest, and you have transformed the house into a chapel for prayer, for intercession. Now your position, whether inside or out, may be defined by its relation to the axis.

The simple device of a walled enclosure with a doorway oriented in a particular direction has established a link between the person (king or god) and the remote. It has established a centre and axis in relation to which the person knows where they are. It has created a spatial hierarchy leading from outside, over the threshold, to inside, to a centre and to the altar positioned opposite the doorway. This is the spatial matrix used in the buildings of many religions.

INTERLUDE: The Woodland Chapel

The Woodland Chapel stands in the grounds of
the Woodland Crematorium on the outskirts of
Stockholm in Sweden. It was designed by Erik
Gunnar Asplund and built around 1918.

Though the building uses more elements than
have yet been introduced in these exercises
– column, rectangular (rather than circular)
walled enclosure, porch and steps (around the
circular heart of the plan) – you can see from
the plan that the design is an exercise in
centre, circle of place and axis. The person too
is an essential ingredient in the architecture
of the building. It is accommodated as corpse
(in a coffin on the rectangular catafalque),
mourner (either sitting around in a circle or
standing paying last respects at the centre),
and priest or officiating officer (speaking at
the altar).

The building is a formalised clearing in the
forest defined by a circle of columns (like an
ancient standing stone circle). An axis, aligned
with the setting sun in the west, is created
by the doorway and an altar in its own hearth-
like niche on the opposite wall. Also on this
axis is the centre of the circle marking the
vertical axis rising to heaven and the generic
position of the mourner saying farewell. The
catafalque is situated in-between the altar and
the vertical axis.

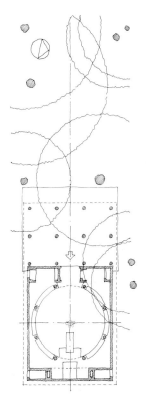

The external appearance of the chapel is a
blend of 'pyramid' (with its allusion to ancient
Egyptian tombs), 'temple' (in the symmetrical
columned portico) and 'cottage in the woods'
(a hint of home and refuge). But the Woodland
Chapel also illustrates the poetic potential of
some of the simple devices by which we can give
form to space through architecture.

You can make an approximation of the
underlying spatial form of interior of the
Woodland Chapel using your blocks and board
(right). You can inhabit it too, with corpse,
mourner and priest, each in the appropriate
place. The spatial form is like the board for
a serious formal 'game' (the funeral ceremony)
with people as players/pieces.

[The Woodland Chapel is one of the Case
Studies in Analysing Architecture.]

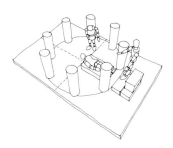

IN YOUR NOTEBOOK...

1 Stonehenge, Salisbury, c.3000 BCE

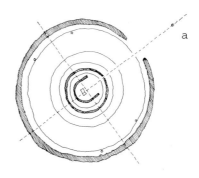

In your notebook... collect examples of axis in space. Study, through redrawing plans, how other architects (from ancient times to the recent present) have employed the axis in the spatial layout of their buildings. Look in particular at the different compositions of centre, circle, enclosure, doorway and axis. Analyse how these compositions provide different positions for the person to occupy (e.g. inside, outside, at the centre, on the threshold, on the axis, at the focus...) and how these different positions relate to or affect the role(s) played by the person and the emotions that person might feel.

Invent your own compositions too. Through drawing, play with different compositions of centre, circle, enclosure, doorway and axis. Establish hierarchies. Experiment with different arrangements. Reflect on the possible relationships of the person with these arrangements. Think of yourself as something like a film director manipulating the identity and emotions of actors. But instead of using the script and verbal instructions you are using spatial prompts engineered by your architectural compositions.

The circle, centre, enclosure, doorway and axis have played an important part in the spatial forms of religious buildings of all faiths. The drawings on this and the following page show the plans of six buildings from different periods of history

Stonehenge consists of a series of concentric circles: six of stones of various sizes surrounded by a seventh which is an earthwork and ditch. The smallest 'circle' is opened into a horseshoe shape in response to the main axis which relates to the point of sunrise on the summer solstice – marked by the hele stone (a) and avenue of approach – and sunset on the winter solstice. Though the circles are permeable (consisting not of walls but of spaced stones) doorways (and hence thresholds) through each are implied on the axis of approach. Near but not quite at the centre of these circles is a stone which is apparently an altar. Its off-centre position allows the actual geometric centre to be occupied by a person, perhaps the priest or holy man officiating at some ceremony or rite.

36

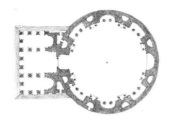

2 Pantheon, Rome, c.126 CE

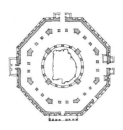

3 Dome of the Rock, Jerusalem, c.690

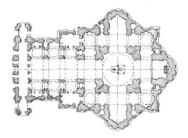

4 St Peter's, Rome, 1506-1626

and of different ideologies. (Although such labels might be open to debate...) Stonehenge was apparently a temple for pagan rites, the Pantheon originally framed a pantheistic religion but later became a Christian building, the Dome of the Rock is Islamic but also sacred to Christians and Jews, St Peter's is Roman Catholic Christian, the Villa Rotonda was built in a Christian context but can be interpreted as a temple to the human being, and Fitzwilliam College Chapel is a small Christian chapel belonging to a university college. Each building provides a (uniting) reference point (datum) for a particular constituency or community of people – stone age tribes, Romans, Muslims, Roman Catholics, humanity, the students of a particular Cambridge college.

All these communities (and more) have found use for the architectural devices of circle of place, centre, enclosure, doorway and axis in giving form to space for occupation and ritual. But each building uses these devices in a different way, with different effects.

Using diagrams (like mine for Stonehenge) analyse each of them. Think, in particular, about what has been positioned at the centre of each and why. Think also about how the other devices (circle, enclosure, doorway, axis) contribute to the overall form given to space in each instance.

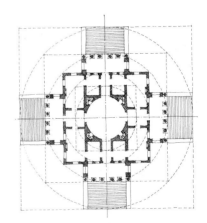

5 Villa Rotonda, Vicenza, 1591

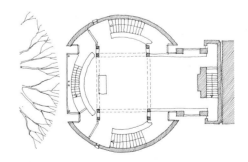

6 Fitzwilliam College Chapel, Cambridge, 1991

(These plans are not to the same scale.)

37

EXERCISE 3e. Lines of doorways.

Make a line of three doorways sharing the
same axis. The axis generated by a doorway,
in conjunction with the person's line
of sight, may be reinforced by making a
sequence of doorways on a shared axis.

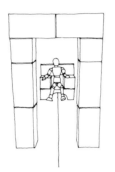
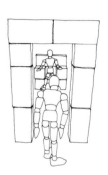

1

We have seen previously in this exercise
that a doorway establishes an axis that
can relate a significant object or person
with another (*1*). To the person standing
before the doorway, the object or person on
the other side exists in 'another world',
and is thereby lent additional importance
and mystery. This otherworldliness may be
enhanced, reinforced, if the significant
object or person is situated beyond not
just one doorway but a sequence (*2*).

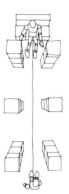

The sequence of doorways creates a
hierarchy of status between the significant
object or person (maybe a queen or
the representation of a god) and the
supplicant. It also creates a sequence of
intermediate 'worlds' of status that grows
as the significant focus is approached.

2

The doorways may also present a sequence
of (psychological or real) barriers through
which persons only of a particular status
may pass.

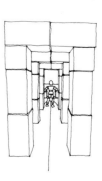

INTERLUDE: lines of doorways

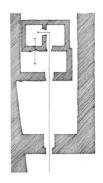

1 Temple of Osiris Hek-Djet, Karnak, c.900 BCE

Sequences of aligned doorways imply progression
in hierarchical stages towards a remote goal or
state of being, or perhaps symbolise regression
into progressively deeper recesses of the
psyche. They elicit feelings of reverence
and aspiration. Lines of doorways are found
in buildings - temples and palaces - through
history and across cultures. The prospect of a
line of doorways can be inviting, challenging,
forbidding... They can imply a sequence of
spaces you might be invited to explore,
challenged to attain or forbidden from entering.

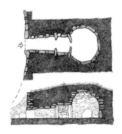

2 Cairn O'Get burial chamber, Scotland, c.3000 BCE

3 Tarxien Temple, Malta, c.3000 BCE

The symbolic power of a line of doorways is
illustrated in a small temple which is part of
the complex of ancient Egyptian buildings at
Karnak (1). In the temple of Osiris Hek-Djet
there is a line of actual doorways through which
a person, maybe only a privileged priest, might
physically pass. These lead to a chamber with
access, at right angles, to an inner chamber
- the culmination of the route. Alongside and
parallel is another sequence of doorways - an
image carved in the surface of the solid stone
wall and appearing to lead into the same inner
chamber. This is a line of doorways, of illusory
extent (because of the perspective) through
which only the souls of the dead may pass.

Lines of doorways can be found in even
older buildings too. Their power must have
been discovered in prehistoric times. They are
evident, for example, in some neolithic burial
chambers (2). They seem to be associated with
ideas of progressive stages towards attaining
a transcendent state of being as in the (much
grander) ancient temples on the island of
Malta, like Tarxien (3). The lines of doorways
culminate in an altar framed within its own
niche or doorway. Some of the altars themselves
are in the form of miniature doorways (4),
indicating that the doorway itself was deemed
spiritually significant. Some of the doorways in
this temple have very high thresholds indicating
that passing through them was seen as something
of a test or rite of passage. The threshold
(as in that of the circle of presence) was
experienced as a transition from one state of
being to another.

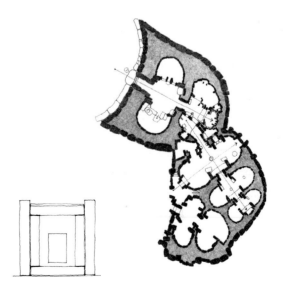

4 An altarpiece in the form of a small doorway

39

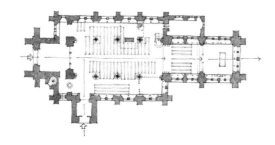

1

A similar progression of doorways and thresholds underpins the organisation of the processional route from west door to altar in a Christian church (1).

Lines of doorways may be associated with emergence as well as penetration. The long line of seven doorways in the Temple of Rameses II (2) might be interpreted as indicating progressive stages of approach towards the culmination of an eighth, false, doorway. But they might also be interpreted as a sequence passed through by the spirit of the resurrected pharaoh as it comes out through the false doorway to re-enter the world of the living.

Sometimes when the Prince of Wales gives televised speeches at St James's Palace in London he stands on a podium at a doorway (3). Behind is a sequence of aligned doorways axially focused on a throne. It is as if the Prince has emerged from his cloistered, twice-detached, royal world to speak to his subjects.

Sequences of doorways do not necessarily imply hierarchical progression. They may relate to transitions from one room or 'world' to another in a sequence.

In Petworth House in England (4) there is a long line of rooms with doorways en filade. They are aligned along one edge of the rooms, adjacent to the windows, leaving the major part of each room to be used for inhabitation (as a circle of place). The doorways take you through a sequence of rooms each with different characters and content.

The composer Frédéric Chopin stayed for a while in an apartment in a monastery at Valldemossa on the island of Mallorca (5). Here the sequence of doorways takes you from a bare and severe monastic corridor, through a small lobby, into the main living apartment, and then through a loggia into a beautiful and sunny formal garden with an elevated panoramic view across the dramatic scenery of northern Mallorca.

[For more on the powers and phenomenology of the doorway see Doorway, Routledge, 2007.]

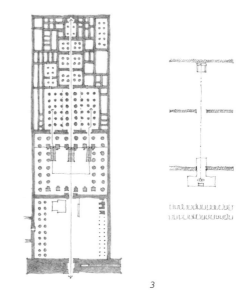

2   *3*

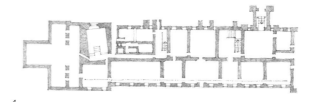

4

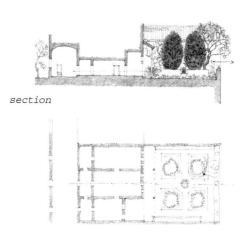

section

5   plan

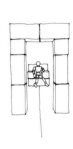

1

EXERCISE 3f. Countering/denying the power of the doorway axis.

The doorway axis is itself powerful and therefore associated with power. It has the power to focus attention on a particular object or personage, the apparent significance of which is thereby enhanced. It is usually associated with a threshold, or sequence of thresholds, which punctuate the person's experience of space, maybe as challenges or as momentary transitions from one place or state of being into another.

2

Sometimes, however, you the architect might want to control, reduce, deny the power of the doorway axis. As in all creative disciplines, things can become more intriguing when a strong, seemingly dominant, theme or idea is challenged, subverted, thwarted.

The relationship between doorway, axis and object of attention (god, personage, altar, work of art...) is a dominant theme in much architecture (1). The first and most obvious way to break that relationship is, of course, to block it: either with a wall (2) which might be inside (as shown) or outside; or by inserting a column on the centre line of the doorway (3). In this arrangement the visitor (the person, you approaching the doorway) can no longer see, or only partially see, the object of attention through the doorway, and has to take a route when entering which deviates

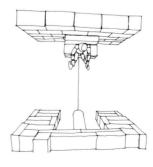
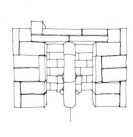

3

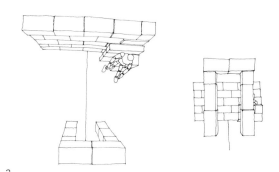

1

from the axial approach. Though blocking
is a method of organising space to deny a
doorway axis, it is not the only one.

One might avoid placing the object of
attention on the dominant axis, either
to one side (1) or maybe in a corner
(2). One might even place it in a corner
beside the doorway (3). Each of these
arrangements, all deviating from adherence
to the dominant doorway axis, results in a
different relationship between the person
(the visitor to the space, whom you must
imagine as yourself in these drawings) and
the object of attention.

Notice how, in response to the
asymmetrical arrangements of 2 and 3, the
design of the 'throne' has been altered
to make it asymmetrical too. Whereas in 4
the throne remains symmetrical, setting up
its own axis (and that of its occupant) in
counterpoint to that of the doorway. 4 is
therefore subtly different from 2.

The permutations are many, and each
possesses its own subtleties in regard
of the relationships between: the person
(visitor); the doorway and its axis; the
room; and the object(s) of attention
within it. With your blocks, on your board
marked with an axis, play with as many
permutations as you can, recording each as
a plan drawing in your notebook.

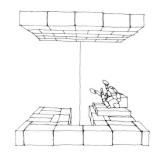

2

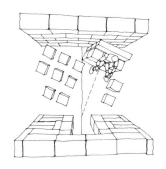

3

4

It would not make sense: 1. to situate the object of attention blocking the doorway; 2. situate the object of attention facing the wall, or 3. into a corner; 4. make the doorway so it does not give access into the room. Try other arrangements of these elements that do not make sense.

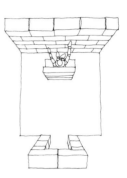

1

EXERCISE 3g. Make a senseless doorway/axis/focus composition.

You may use walls as instruments for manipulating (playing with) relationships between person, doorway, axis, room and object of attention. Some 'senseless' examples are illustrated alongside.

Playing with the spatial relationships between elements like this is similar to a grammatical exercise in language. As in language there is no one right structure for a sentence. Some arrangements are simple and direct. Some are complex and subtle. But, as in language, all should make sense (unless for some contrary poetic reason). Some arrangements may be 'wrong' because they do not make sense. Sense is, as in language, something you must learn to recognise and judge.

Making something senseless can help you understand and recognise sense. In the case of this exercise the aim is to develop your understanding of spatial arrangement. Children already have this understanding intuitively; e.g. when they recognise the significance of sitting at the head of the table or purposefully step beyond a threshold to challenge parental authority. To become an architect you must consciously develop this understanding – develop your sense of spatial sense – so that you can use it in various and subtle ways.

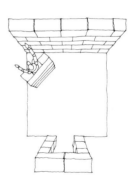

2

3

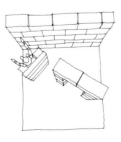

4

IN YOUR NOTEBOOK...

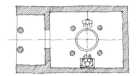

In your notebook... collect examples where
an architect has contradicted (countered,
distorted, denied, deflected, avoided...)
an axis in space. Look for examples in
the buildings you experience but also
look in architectural journals and books.
Contradicting an axis is not the same as
ignoring one. You are looking for conscious
intent on the part of the architect to:
set up an axis and then deviate from it;
deflect an axis that is already there; or
resolve two axes that are not aligned or
congruent. This may involve wanting to deny
the implicit power of the axis or allowing
another force or influence to deflect or
distort an axis. Here are some examples.

*The throne of a king in ancient Greece was to
one side of the doorway axis. This may have been
to avoid a confrontational relationship with
something sacred to which the axis was oriented
or, with a visitor entering, to avoid the glare
of bright light from the doorway.*

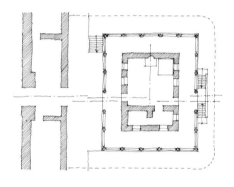

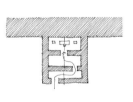

*In ancient Egypt some mortuary temples were
built with doorways deviating from the axis
of the altar (above left). This may have been
to avoid the altar being visible from outside
(to break a line of sight) or to stop spirits
escaping back into the world of the living (to
disturb a line of passage).*

*Spatial sense can be related to ideological or
philosophical sense. In the Hall of Audiences
at Topkapi Palace in Istanbul, the relationship
between Sultan and supplicant is managed by the
arrangement of doorway axes. No person occupies
the axis (associated with power) so the Sultan
– the object of attention – and the supplicant
are situated in corners. Only the hearth is
positioned on the central axis of the Hall.
(See Doorway, pages 54-55.)*

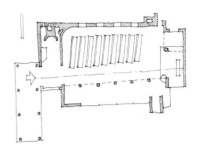

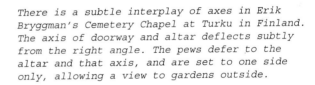

In Isfahan the axis of the main square deflects to find that of the great mosque which indicates the direction of Mecca.

There is a subtle interplay of axes in Erik Bryggman's Cemetery Chapel at Turku in Finland. The axis of doorway and altar deflects subtly from the right angle. The pews defer to the altar and that axis, and are set to one side only, allowing a view to gardens outside.

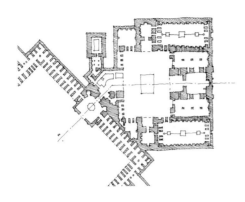

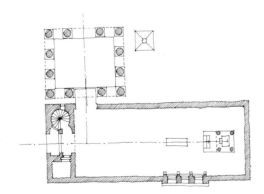

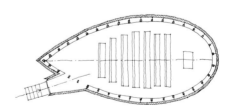

Many churches are entered from one side, usually the south, of the main axis of the altar. In Sigurd Lewerentz's Chapel of the Resurrection in Stockholm entrance is from the north, the direction associated with death. Exit is through another doorway, along the axis towards the setting sun.

The tear drop shape of Peter Zumthor's chapel at Song Benedikt in Switzerland relates to the axis of the altar and pews. The doorway avoids that axis.

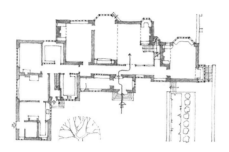

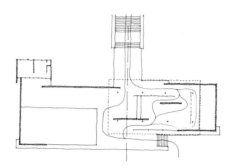

When the Arts and Crafts architect M.H. Baillie Scott designed Blackwell, a house in the English Lake District, he could have arranged the entrance so that the doorways shared a single axis between the courtyard and the main room. Instead he shifted subsequent doorways off the axis of the first, outside, main doorway, making the visitor's experience of the entrance less formal, less grand, more like the entrance of an English medieval house.

In his Barcelona Pavilion, Mies van der Rohe contradicted the axis (denied the axis its power) by 'crossing it out' with a wall. This had the effect of ensuring that visitors would wander through its simple labyrinth of spaces. (The Barcelona Pavilion is one of the subjects of analysis in Twenty Buildings Every Architect Should Understand.)

SUMMARY OF SECTION ONE

In the exercises of this first Section we have seen that architecture is about giving form. Through architecture we give form to material and to space – the substance without substance. We tend to think of giving form to material as being about making objects: we mould clay into a model; we form dough into a loaf of bread; we form soldiers into lines of defence. But architecture is more complex. It gives form to space – the intangible – too.

If we see a building as an object, the person is cast as a spectator, admiring or hating what is seen. When architecture gives form to space, the person is an ingredient, taken through a variety of experiences, completing the architecture with their presence and viewpoint.

When we think of buildings as objects, architecture deals in appearance, three-dimensional (sculptural) composition..., maybe symbolic allusions or associations (e.g. buildings that 'look like' pyramids, temples, cottages, or amoebic blobs...). When we conceive architecture as giving form to space, we are setting the spatial matrix within which life is lived. The architecture of space accommodates the person and establishes a frame for behaviour, relationships and experience.

In the block models you have built so far, you have seen the power of the centre, the circle of place and the threshold. You have also seen how a conjunction of eye and doorway projects an axis that can establish linkage between the near and the remote, between the person and something within or out in the distance.

In its dealing in space, architecture is philosophical, i.e. it makes sense of things. In your models you have seen two ways in which giving form to space sets a matrix by which we make sense of our lives. The hearth provides a centre around which daily life revolves. The house with its furniture provides an ordered layout that makes sense, spatially, of what we do in our domestic setting; it establishes places for the various things we do in our daily lives. The layout of a building's plan is a descriptive account, manifest spatially, of a way to live. This is a non-verbal kind of pragmatic everyday philosophy. The pragmatic organisation of places relates to and provides the framework for activities, ceremonies and relationships.

In the temple, with its axis (whether Stonehenge or Fitzwilliam College Chapel), the spatial form attains to the level of a religious creed. It offers a grand philosophy by which to make sense of things spiritual. The centre provides a focus of attention – maybe an altar – a reference point to which the rest of the world relates. The circle defines a sacred area within which ceremonies may be performed. The axis relates the centre, or adjacent altar, to the remote and provides a datum by which the person may know where they are. And the doorway threshold, whilst defining a distinction between inside and outside, stimulates a (reverential) frisson of transition from the ordinary everyday world outside into the special (sacred) place inside. The threshold also defines the line between inclusion (being a member) and exclusion (being not a member, a foreigner, alien, exile...).

In these early exercises we have seen that doorways are powerful. We have aligned them to create a hierarchy of spaces or a sequence of different places that lead the person through a series of experiences (rooms). Doorways tantalise and draw the person on; they stimulate aspiration - wanting to get from one place into the next, and then the next.

We have also seen that the axis of a doorway or series of aligned doorways can feel too powerful, needing to be countered by blocking, avoidance or deflection.

In Section One we have seen the existential geometry of the circle of place, of the centre and the axis. In the next section we shall experiment with the various geometries of architecture and the conflicts and harmonies that can arise between them.

Section Two
GEOMETRY

Section Two
GEOMETRY

This second set of exercises focuses on the different geometries affecting architecture. Each of the ingredients of architecture has its own geometry. The world in which the products of architecture are built has, in its usual interpretation, a geometry of six directions. These are: east (where the sun rises); south (where the sun, at noon, is at its highest); west (where the sun sets); and north (where the sun never goes). (For the southern hemisphere, reverse the descriptions of north and south.) In addition, there are the vertical directions of down (the direction in which gravity exerts its force) and up (the direction of the sky above).

The person living on the surface of the earth can also be interpreted as having six directions: front (or forward); back (or backward); left (sideways); right (sideways); down; and up. The person projects the axis – from its eyes – of the line of sight; and, being able to move, the line of passage. Though people come in different shapes and sizes, the majority fit into a fairly limited range. The extent of a person's movement – pace, step up or down, reach, span (of arms or hand)... – also falls into a fairly narrow range. All these constitute the geometry of the person.

When people come together as groups they form patterns. This is social geometry. In that architecture sets the frames for what we do, it may respond to or set such social geometry in physical and spatial form.

The built form by which architecture is realised, and which (usually) mediates between the person and world, also has its geometries. These will be explored in the following exercises but they include, especially, the geometry of making (the ways in which the forms, properties and characteristics of building materials can influence the forms built from them) and the related geometry of planning.

The aspiration to ideal geometry – the imposition of perfect geometric figures – square, circle... cube, sphere... – onto architectural form – will be the subject of later exercises in this section.

Some of the geometries of being have been touched upon already in these exercises: the circle with its centre; the four horizontal directions associated with the axis (line of sight); the geometry of the person. Further discussion of the various geometries affecting architecture can be found in Analysing Architecture, 'Geometries of Being'.

Sometimes these architectural geometries are in harmony, sometimes they are in conflict. In a work of architecture it is rare to be able to achieve a harmony between all the different kinds of geometry. In due course we shall look at some instances where this does happen.

EXERCISE 4: alignment

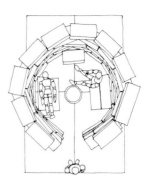

In this exercise, using your board, blocks and person(s), you will model the geometries of the world and of the person. You will also experience some of the restrictions/conditions that the geometry of making imposes on building (i.e. realising works of architecture in physical – material and spatial – form). Your simple wooden blocks are not real building materials but they do share some characteristics with proprietary materials available for constructing real buildings that must stand on the ground under the force of gravity. The chief of these characteristics relate to the blocks' geometry: their (precise) rectangular form; their standardised dimensions; and their simple proportions of 1:1, 1:2, 1:3...

We can use the circular house built in Exercise 2 to explore the different sorts of geometry that compete for attention and dominance in architecture.

EXERCISE 4a. Geometries of the world and person.

Without the house your board has its own geometry. It has four sides; it is rectangular; its opposite sides are parallel; its corners are right angles; it is flat and horizontal.

Your board also has a centre around which a circle of place might be drawn.

With the two axes indicating the four cardinal directions your board can be seen as a simple diagram of the world.

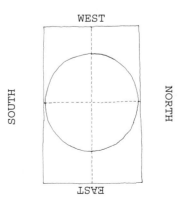

Your person has its geometry too.

The person has four aspects: front; back; left; and right, which project axes in each of the four directions. It also has an 'up' direction, stretching into the sky; and a 'down' pressing into the ground, the direction of the pull of gravity.

The person is its own, mobile, centre, around which the person's own circle of place may be drawn.

EXERCISE 4b. Geometries aligned.

Position your person on the board, at its centre, so that its geometry is aligned with that of the board.

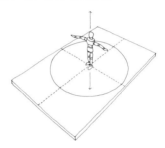

This alignment, between the geometry of the person and that of the board, may be achieved whether the person is standing or lying down.

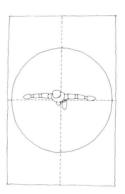 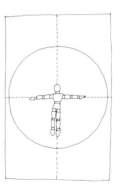

The centres, axes and circles of place of the person and of the board coincide.

And, since the board is a simple model of the world, we can see that there are

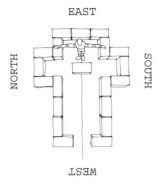

EAST

NORTH

SOUTH

WEST

A Christian church is an alignment of the geometry of the crucifix – which represents the geometry of a person – the geometry of the altar, the geometry of the building and, since the building is oriented east-west, the geometry of the world.

situations where the geometry of the person can be aligned with that of the world. (It might be argued that we interpret the world around us in terms of our own geometry.)

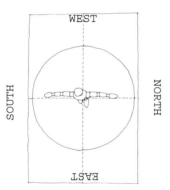

WEST

SOUTH

NORTH

EAST

That alignment of geometries might be between the person and the cardinal directions – north, south, east, west – but it may also be achieved in relation to some other datum: the sea with its distant horizon; a wall (the Western Wall in Jerusalem, for example); a remote focus (the Ka'ba in Mecca, for example); or just the street outside your house.

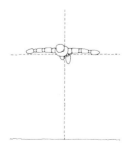

EXERCISE 4c. Architecture as an instrument of alignment.

You can see then that when you rebuild your wall around the circle of place, leaving a doorway for access, you are creating an instrument that physically records and reinforces the alignment between the four-directional horizontal geometry of the person and the four-directional horizontal geometry we ascribe to the world.

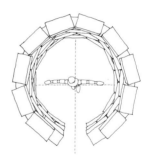

But whereas the person will move around and away, the geometry manifest in the building persists as a record and reminder of that alignment.

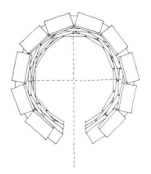

53

IN YOUR NOTEBOOK...

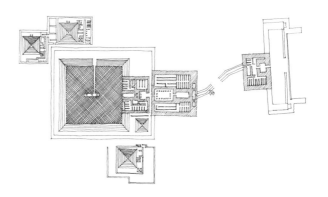

Since ancient times buildings regarded as sacred have been designed as instruments of alignment. The square sides of ancient pyramids, like compasses, were aligned north-east-south-west. The east was the direction of life – the rising sun and the river Nile; south is the direction of the sun at its height; west is the direction of the setting sun and the great expanse of the lifeless desert; and north is the sunless direction.

In your notebook... collect examples where architecture acts as an instrument of alignment. You should draw your examples as plans, simplified if you wish. Your examples should include those in which architecture aligns the person with the world and others where the architecture aligns the person with something else. You can find some examples in books on architectural history but you should also find some more recent examples, maybe in current architectural magazines, and examples from your own everyday life.

You have probably experienced the aligning power of architecture in your everyday life more often than you consciously acknowledge. For example, your own house might be aligned, through the orientation of its main doorway and windows, to: the sun in the south (north, in the southern hemisphere); a view of the sea and its distant horizon; the public road outside... You have also experienced the aligning power of architecture every time you have sat in a classroom, lecture room, theatre, cinema or even dining room.

Place-making and alignment (orientation) are two fundamental powers of architecture. It is no wonder you find them in grand public architecture too. These powers belong to churches, mosques and temples of all religions and faiths. They also belong to palaces, parliaments, factories and workshops.

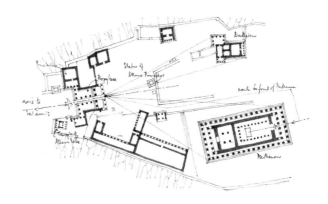

The principal buildings on the Acropolis in Athens are instruments of alignment. The Parthenon – the main temple to Athena, patron goddess of Athens – is aligned to the rising sun in the east. The Propylaea – the entrance into the sanctuary – is aligned with Athena's birthplace on the distant island of Salamis.

Mecca

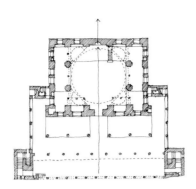

A mosque aligns worshippers with Mecca.

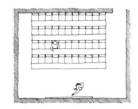

A lecture room (theatre, cinema...) is an instrument of alignment, aligning the audience to sit facing the lecturer (play, movie...).

NORTH

WEST

EAST

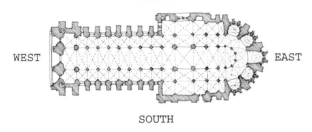

SOUTH

A church aligns the congregation to the altar and the cardinal directions of the world.

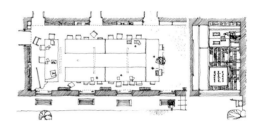

A table for a meeting is an instrument of alignment, as may also be the room in which it stands. (This is a drawing of the room in which I was sitting during a long meeting. The portion at the right is a section turned sideways. The tables and chairs set the frame within which the meeting took place. The chair person is at the left of the drawing aligned with the axis of the tables, which is parallel with but not quite aligned with that of the room - to allow people to walk down one side of the table. Notice that even the benches outside are aligned with the geometry of the room and its windows. This is a certain kind of neatness.

NORTH

WEST

EAST

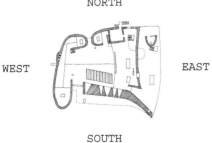

SOUTH

Even Le Corbusier's chapel at Ronchamp is an instrument of alignment, though its own geometry is not rectangular.

EXERCISE 5: anthropometry

Architecture accommodates many different kinds of thing - animals, works of art, furniture, even atmospheres or moods... - but its chief and most challenging content is us, people. Human beings can see (in straight lines) and have emotional responses to changing situations. We also have physical form. Though people come in all shapes and sizes, these variations fall within a fairly narrow range. Human beings rarely exceed a particular height, and generally they move, their joints bend, in the same way. The body - its size, reach, mobility - presents another kind of geometry - anthropometry - which can be distinguished from the four-directional geometry we ascribe to the world around and the geometry of the four aspects of the person standing in space (both of which geometries were the subject of Exercise 4). Anthropometry (the measure of the person) is a third geometric factor to be taken into account when giving form to space through architecture.

EXERCISE 5a. A big enough bed.

You will have noticed, in the house I designed in Exercise 2 (and in my rough model of Asplund's Woodland Chapel, on page 35), that the beds (and catafalque) would not be comfortable for the people (or corpse) shown: their heads and feet (coffin) would dangle over the ends.

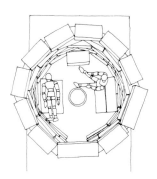

The beds are not long enough; if they had been they would have occupied too much of the space available within the circle of wall. Though not in a real building, this is an example of a conflict of geometries. In this case it was caused by a combination of: the standard sizes of the building blocks available; the size of the little artists' manikins I was using for 'the person'; and the size of circle I could draw on my board.

I could have made the beds long enough for the manikins but then they would have

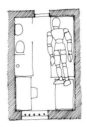

taken up too much of the limited interior space. It would not be acceptable to make such a compromise in a real building. How could you mitigate the problem?

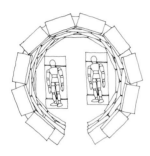

Being no more than an indicative model, the conflict was 'unreal' and I offered a compromise using a smaller bed. But such conflicts afflict real products of architecture too, buildings that have to accommodate the actual size of human beings.

The range of sizes catered for in building elements is not always generous enough. Prison accommodation, for example, usually tends to be economical with space. In January 2011 it was reported in the media that a Dutch prisoner was going to court because his cell was too small for him. His bed was 770mm (2'6") wide by 1960mm (6'5") long, which would be large enough for most of the human race. But this prisoner, described by his lawyer as 'a giant', was 1000mm (3'3") wide by 2070mm (6'9") long. He was complaining that he could not use the lavatory or shower properly either.

The offices of Members of the Scottish Parliament (designed by Enric Miralles and opened in 2004) have window seats tailored to the size of a person. The seat and steps allow the Member to adopt various positions, from sitting upright to reclining with feet up. The window seats were intended for Members to sit and ponder.

EXERCISE 5b. Some key points of measure.

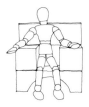

The bed, where we lie down to sleep, is one of the key situations where we measure our bodies against the architecture that accommodates us. There are others.

Use your building blocks to explore the relationship between the size of the body and various components in the spaces we occupy. Within the limits of the blocks you have and the size of the manikin you are using to represent yourself and other human beings try to find harmonic relationships between the person and the following: a step or series of steps; a seat; a work desk or dining table; a counter for selling or preparing food; a doorway...

You can experiment to find heights that are too low, too high and just right. In the case of the doorway you can decide on the apt width as well as height. It is no accident that the height and width of a doorway is similar to the length and breadth of a bed; they both accommodate the human form, with some leeway in both the long and short dimensions.

You might also muse on when it could be appropriate to exaggerate the height of a step or doorway; maybe to exaggerate the status of the person (or god) who might use (or be imagined to use) them. (See pages 138-139 of *Analysing Architecture*, 3rd edition.)

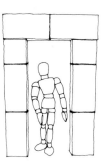

IN YOUR NOTEBOOK...

In your notebook... measure and draw elements of buildings that relate to the sizes of people. Many of these elements are made to standard dimensions; others tend to be found within a limited range. For example: 'off-the-shelf' doors are made to a range of standard widths and heights; dining chairs tend to be similar heights; as are tables and desks, or work counters for kitchens. Steps in public buildings tend to be shallower than those in private houses.

By your researches, as well as by looking at manufacturers' catalogues, discover the size ranges of these elements that relate to the sizes of people. Estimate the tolerances involved. Try them for yourself; get a conscious feel for their dimensions. As an architect, these dimensions are part of the language with which you work. They should become readily available to you from your memory.

This may seem a prosaic aspect of architecture but the dimensions of elements that relate to the sizes of people constitute an important way in which the form that is given to space engages with the people who occupy that space. There can be a comfortable agreement between the geometry of people and the geometry of built elements, or an uncomfortable conflict. Poetry and harmony can be instilled into the subtle manipulation of scale.

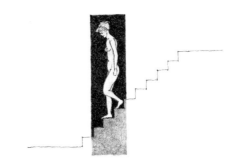

The ways people move relate to spaces they occupy. The sizes of basic elements such as steps and stairs respond to the innate dimensions of the human frame and of its capacity for movement.

EXERCISE 6: social geometry

Architecture does not only accommodate the individual person; it accommodates people in congregation too. And when they congregate people arrange themselves in particular geometries. Architecture - the giving of form to space - responds to and sets these social geometries.

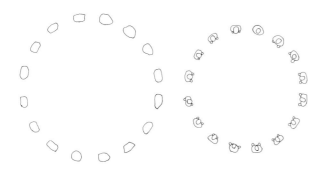

As well as identifying a centre, a circle of place and perhaps the geometry of the world, a circle of standing stones may also be interpreted as manifesting the geometry of a group of people standing together, maybe witnessing a ceremony.

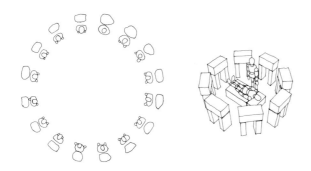

EXERCISE 6a. The social geometry of a circular house.

The spatial arrangement of our circular house establishes a social geometry between the two occupants. With the beds at each side of the fire they can sit opposite each other talking while warming their feet.

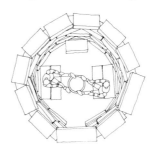

    The two beds have an equal relationship to both the fire and the table (altar).
    If someone were to enter, there would be an equal relationship between each of the occupants sitting on their beds and the visitor, demonstrating a social triangle between the beds and the doorway (which expands into a quadrangle if the 'altar' is included).

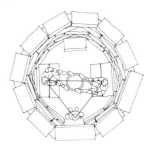

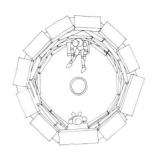

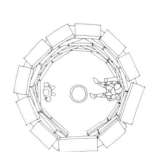

Try other social arrangements within the circular house. The circle, which in other ways can be impractical, lends itself to various arrangements of social geometry. We have seen (in Exercise 3) that the doorway axis creates a significant position on the wall opposite. Sitting there you (your person) hold a dominant position. Anyone who enters will be in direct confrontation (1). Imagine yourself as the person entering.

As the person occupying the throne you may prefer to sit to one side of the doorway axis. In this position a visitor (supplicant) would enter from your side and, when standing opposite, occupy a position of greater equality, with both of you equally lit by the light from the doorway (2).

The circle lends itself to a gathering of people too, assembled maybe to discuss matters of shared interest. In the circle all are, more or less, equal (3).

A person entering through the doorway into such a gathering would be like an actor coming onto stage in front of an audience (4). Though the 'stage' area would be small this arrangement is very like a theatre, with the doorway as a proscenium arch. It is also like a church, with the doorway as chancel arch; or like a mosque, with the doorway as *mihrab*.

1

2

3

4

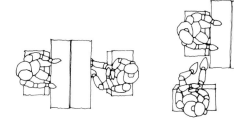

EXERCISE 6b. Other situations in which architecture frames social geometry.

1

Reflect on how arrangements of people can have emotional effects on those involved, affecting their perception of their situation and of relationships with others.

As we have already seen in Marina Abramovic's 'The Artist is Present' (page 27) and in the Notebook Exercise on 'aligning geometries' (page 54), a table can be an instrument for establishing social geometry. In 'The Artist is Present', the table intercedes in the confrontation between Abramovic and her visitor. A longitudinal dining table establishes relationships between the dominant positions at each end, seats next to the ends, and those in the middle of each side (1). In Roman times the social geometry of dining was rather different. Guests reclined on couches in a *triclinium* (2), reaching food from a table in the centre.

Doctors, in their consultation rooms, usually avoid the confrontation implied by sitting behind a desk by arranging their furniture so that patients sit to one side (3).

A doorway (4) frames a point where people meet. It acts as a fulcrum between the two worlds they occupy and channels the line of eye contact.

2

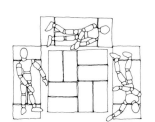

3

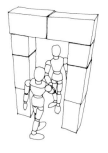

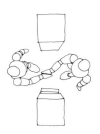

4

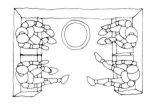
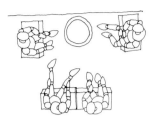
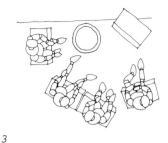

1   2   3

A traditional ingle-nook frames social geometry around a hearth (1). A television placed in a room distorts the social geometry of furniture arranged around a hearth (2, 3).

There are many ways in which architecture sets the frame, perhaps a matrix, for the positions and relationships of people in groups. The layout of the lecture room (page 55) is one example. So too is the layout of beds in a hospital ward (4), oriented towards a central aisle, or that of graves in a cemetery (5) oriented towards the setting sun, Mecca or the sea.

Various architectural elements can be used as instruments for managing, framing, accommodating social geometries. These may be beds, chairs, a table, desks, a hearth, a television...; doorways, walls, roofs, windows, pathways (aisles, corridors, roads...) all play a part too.

4

On the beach a rug might be an instrument of social geometry. Though if it is too small the geometry it produces might be a little perverse.

5

INTERLUDE: choir stall

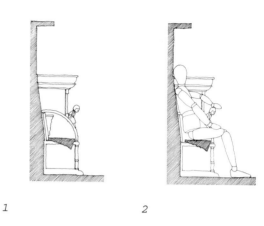

1   2

Cathedrals have choir stalls. In some cases
individual stalls are designed to accommodate
the human form in a variety of positions. They
are designed according to the anthropometry
of sitting, standing and half-sitting/half-
standing. This is done with: a seat that folds
up or down, fitted with a smaller perch - a
misericord - on its under side; knobs (maybe
in the form of cherubs) useful in standing up;
and ledges on which to lean when standing.
Some choristers might be aged and infirm, and
all these would be helpful and make them more
comfortable when responding to the liturgical
demands of a service.

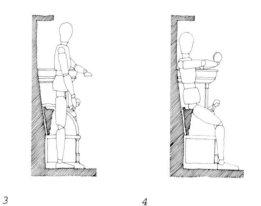

3   4

   When the seat is down (1) the stall
accommodates normal sitting. The knob helps the
chorister lever himself into a standing position
(2). When standing, the ledges (3, at elbow
height) provide the chorister with something on
which to lean, making it easier to stand for a
long time by reducing the weight on the feet.
And the misericord provides a surreptitious
perch for those who need it, so they may appear
standing whilst actually supporting their weight
on the small seat (4).

   A choir is also an example of architecture
providing the frame for social geometry (5).
Choristers are seated in a regular arrangement
of stalls, oriented as a group towards the altar
(not shown in the drawing).

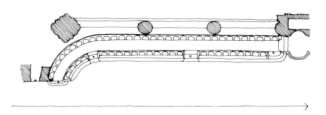

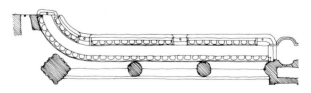

5

IN YOUR NOTEBOOK...

In your notebook... think of and find other situations in which architecture frames social geometries. Find examples that correspond to those you have experimented with in your block models. Be open to finding others too. Social geometries begin with the patterns people make when they come together for various communal activities. Architecture frames these patterns but also modifies them, tidies them up, orders them... makes sense of them spatially.

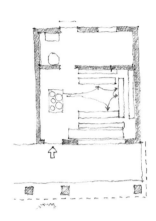

This tiny restaurant in Kerala, South India, frames the social geometry of people eating whilst being served by the cook.

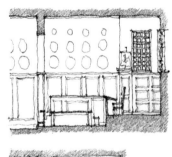

section

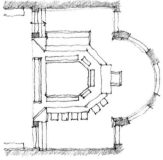

plan

A law court frames the process of hearing and justice. Each player - judge, lawyers, defendant, jury, witness... - is allocated their own precise location within the spatial matrix established by the architecture.

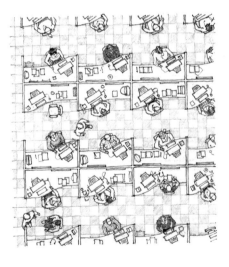

Call centres, where many people work answering questions on the telephone, are carefully arranged to optimise the use of space and the layout of cables. A geometric arrangement is most economical. Desks are designed to suit the relationship between person and computer, with screens to reduce the temptation to gossip with neighbours.

EXERCISE 7: the geometry of making

All the models you have made so far with your blocks have been conditioned by two things: the constant vertical force of gravity acting perpendicular to the horizontal surface of your board (1); and, the regular rectangular geometry of the blocks themselves, probably ordered according to a shared module (2); i.e. blocks are proportioned 1:1, 0.5:2, 1:2, 0.5:3. Gravity and the geometry of building components constitute the basic conditions of the geometry of making.

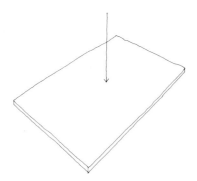

1

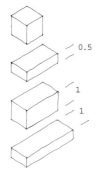

2

EXERCISE 7a. Form and the geometry of building components.

In Exercise 2 we built a circular house. We can now evaluate it, or at least its enclosing wall, in terms of the geometry of making.

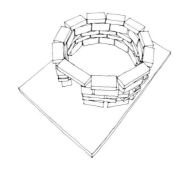

The board provided a flat and horizontal surface on which to build. The flat and parallel opposite surfaces of the rectangular blocks allowed them to rest stable on the board and for a number of courses to be built one upon another. You used blocks of various lengths so that you could 'bond' them – place each block resting on two, i.e. across a joint in the course below – for greater stability. The length of the longest block (0.5:3) determined the width of the doorway. These are all aspects of the geometry of making: the vertical wall in response to the verticality of gravity; the regular courses related to the dimensions of the blocks; the bonded courses for stability; and the

width of the doorway related to the length of its lintel. But there is one aspect in which the geometry of making of this enclosing circular wall was a compromise. If you look at the wall from above, when seen most nearly as a perfect circle, you can see that the arrangement of rectangular blocks is not as neat and regular as could be. Like square pegs and round holes, there is a misfit between rectangular blocks and circular walls. On the inside the joints are very narrow, whilst on the outside they are excessively wide. Blocks are not malleable, they cannot be bent into shape, so to form a circle there has to be compromise.

To build a neat circular wall we could cut each block to shape: parallel top and bottom surfaces but segmental - to the same radius - in plan. You can do this if you have the time to cut each block to shape.

for a wall with this particular radius. They are special not standard. They cannot be used generally, only in particular circumstances. We could built a neat curved wall, wavy in plan, with the same blocks (above). But building a straight flat wall with them would be just as problematic as building a circular wall with rectangular blocks.

Regular rectangular blocks may be used to build neat straight flat walls of any length and to make enclosures of any size.

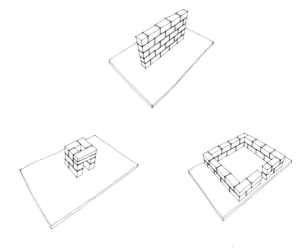

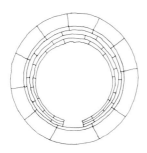

Segmental blocks produce a neat circular wall. But these blocks may only be used

This means that with a stock of regular sized rectangular blocks you can build

Mud or clay bricks might be made with different dimensions in different cultures but their regular rectangular shape and consistent size make building a variety of different sized walls and enclosures easier.

walls of enclosures of almost any size. You do not need specially cut shapes. This is the thinking, done thousands of years ago, behind the basic, consistently sized, clay or mud brick and the cutting of stone into regular rectangular blocks for building walls in ashlar.

Experiment with the neat forms you are able to build using your rectangular blocks. Notice how important your flat horizontal board is as a base for building. If it slopes your walls are no longer vertical - no longer aligned with the vertical force of gravity - and, if the slope is excessive, will not stand. If your base were to be bumpy you would not be able to construct even horizontal courses and your wall would be untidy or even unstable.

EXERCISE 7b. Putting a roof or upper floor on your walls.

Now try to put a roof on your circular house. A flat roof will do, for the moment; you can also think of it as an upstairs floor. You need to make the roof or floor in two layers: a structure of beams; and then the roof or floor itself.

First you will need to span beams from one side of the circle to the other. You might need to cut some pieces of timber to length or you could glue some of the smaller blocks together.

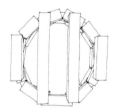

Next you can span some of the smaller blocks from one beam to another, like roof- or floorboards. Though not all exactly the same, roofs and floors around the world are built according to this geometry of making.

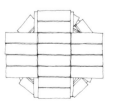

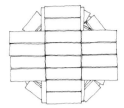

 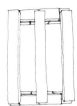 

But you can see straight away that there are problems. The beams have to be cut to different lengths, and the boards (certainly in our simplified example) do not neatly cover the circle; there are small sections that are not covered. The same problems, though not insuperable, afflict real building too. It is fiddly to cover a circular space with intrinsically rectangular elements.

In Exercise 2 I suggested that a circular house could be covered with a conical roof, pitched to shed rain.

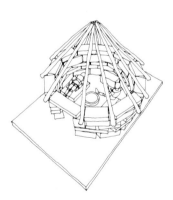

Circular houses since ancient times have been roofed in this or similar ways. It does however require intricacy in design and substantial skill in the builders to do it in more than a rudimentary way. It also would require rather more structure than shown here - to tie the rafters (shown in the drawing) together as an integrated structure.

EXERCISE 7c. Parallel walls.

Now try putting the same sort of roof over a pair of parallel walls.

You can see that the result is neater and easier to achieve. Beams can all be cut or made to the same length and planks can be made in standard lengths. This principle of the geometry of making is the reason why the house in which you live has probably (though not certainly) got rectangular rooms (though floorboards will not be cut to span just between two beams but across a number). The principle illustrated in this exercise applies (broadly speaking) in concrete and steel structures as well as timber.

Of course flat roofs leak in the rain unless they are very carefully waterproofed. But the same basic principle is equally applicable to the provision of roof trusses to support a pitched roof. (See the following Interlude.)

INTERLUDE: a Welsh house

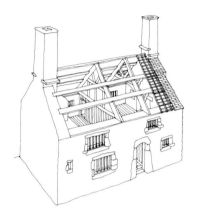

The drawing alongside shows a late seventeenth or early eighteenth century Welsh house. Its walls are built of stone and its floors, roof structure, internal partition walls, doors and windows are in timber. Since glass was not readily available when the house was built, the windows were originally barred for security with vertical pieces of timber and could be shuttered on the inside to keep out the weather.

Part of the roof covering has been cut away in the drawing. You can see that, although the house frames a place to live (divided into a number of rooms on two floors), its form is conditioned throughout by the geometry of making. The walls are parallel, allowing two roof trusses to span from one side to the other. The nearer of these also determines the position of one of the timber partition walls upstairs. The trusses, together with the gable walls, support two purlins on each side which in turn support the common rafters which are arranged parallel along the whole length of the roof. The rafters, in their turn, support battens to which the roof slates are fixed.

You can just see that the internal walls, the upper floor and the windows are all conditioned, in their form, by the geometry of making. The only place where there is some (what might be called) 'aesthetic' geometry is in the small diagonal wind braces - not all are shown in the drawing - at the junctions between the trusses and the purlins. These help to stiffen the structure against the wind. They have been 'cusped' (the 'bites' taken out of their sides) for decoration. Some of the timbers making up the trusses have been cusped too.

The lower drawing is a typical floor plan of such a house. The walls are thick partly for stability because the stones from which they are built are irregular, not like your building blocks. The dotted line across the largest room

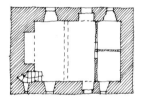

indicates the position of the main beam of the floor above. This supports secondary beams at right angles to which the floorboards are fixed. The stair is in the bottom left corner next to the fireplace. The window jambs (sides) are splayed to admit more light whilst keeping the openings small.

[These drawings are based on illustrations in Peter Smith – Houses of the Welsh Countryside, 1975.]

70

AN OBSERVATION: regarding the circle

Architecture is an arena in which different sorts of geometry vie for preference. It is not a battleground, because geometries cannot fight. But together these different sorts of geometry present the architect with choice, options as to which should prevail in a design.

The geometries we have identified so far (we have not yet identified all of them) in these exercises include:

• the **circle of place** with its **centre**;

• the **geometry of the world** with its four horizontal and two vertical directions;

• the **geometry of the person** (as a whole, with its four directions...);

• the **axis** generated by a **doorway**;

• the geometry of **alignment**;

• **anthropometry** (the geometry of the parts and mobility of the person);

• **social geometry** (the geometry of people together);

• and the **geometry of making** (relating to the dimensions of building components and consistent force of gravity).

We have two (at least) more kinds of geometry to look at in the following exercises: **ideal** geometry; and **complex**, layered, morphed, distorted... geometries.

When we analyse a work of architecture we see that these geometries overlap and rub up against each other, sometimes conflicting, sometimes resonating, sometimes appearing to exist in separate realms. It is rare to be able to get all architecture's various geometries to work harmoniously together. So a work of architecture manifests the preferences, the choices made by the architect to give priority to one or more of these types of geometry.

With these things in mind, we can now assess the circle as an architectural plan form. In our recent exercises it has encountered a few problems. It may represent well the circle of place with its focal centre. It may relate well to the geometry of the person with its four horizontal and two vertical directions, and with eyes in a head that can swivel to survey the world panoramically. The circle may also relate well to the social geometry of people in a group. But we have now seen that the circle encounters problems both with the geometry of the furniture it might need to accommodate and with the geometry of making.

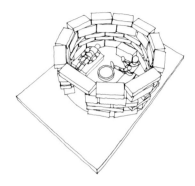

EXERCISE 7d. Now redesign the circular house...

... taking into account the various kinds of geometry, especially the geometry of making.

The circular house (*1*) was an accurate intuitive manifestation of a circle of place in which to live. Its central hearth was the centre of a small domestic realm insulated by a wall from the world around with all its tribulations and threats. But the furniture did not fit and, taking into account the geometry of making, there are easier, more sensible, ways to build and roof a building.

Now rebuild the house in the way that your rectangular bricks 'want' you to build it and in a way that will be easy to roof (with either a flat or pitched roof); i.e. as a rectangle (*2*). Though there are issues to think about with regard to bonding the blocks – so that each rests on two (over a joint) in the course below – the result is neater and better resolved. The furniture, at a size suited to the inhabitants, also fits; there is harmony between the rectangular bed and the rectangular room.

The central hearth does however get in the way, so let's move it to a fireplace at the far end (*3*). The inhabitants can put tables in the corners at the feet of their beds if they wish. The doorway is rather exposed too, so let's add a protecting

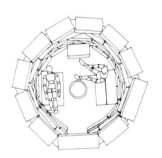

1

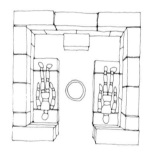

2

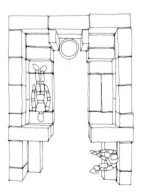

3

The plan of Walter Pichler's Chapel for the Great Cross (right, 1978-79) illustrates the rectangular enclosure's relationship with the four directions. In its Christian symbolism it also shows the poetic potential of this relationship.

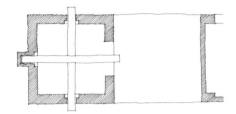

porch by extending the parallel side walls. This might make a pleasant place to sit in the morning sun or to sleep on a hot night. The house is still very basic but it is neater as a rectangle than as a circle.

In this simple rectangular house the doorway axis is just as powerful as it was in the circular house, if not more so.

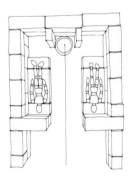

The rectangle also seems to respond more strongly to the four aspects of the person and the four horizontal directions of the

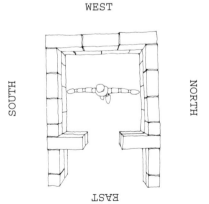

world. Even if the person moves around there is always that four-directional datum to relate to; it is known as the 'quadrature', and is a powerful theme in the architectures of cultures around the world.

It would be understandable to orient the house with its doorway towards the sun rising in the morning, so that the light would warm and wake. Then its other walls would relate to the north, south and west. Doing this, the rectangular house becomes a frame that mediates and orients the person in relation to the world, the horizon, the rhythms of day and night. There must be some psychological attraction to the way in which the architecture of a simple building can *place* the person in relation to space and time.

Incidentally, I'm not sure why the inhabitants of my rectangular house are lying on their beds with their heads towards the doorway. They could equally be the other way, with their heads by the fire. Which would you prefer?

A house with a north facing doorway would feel different from one with its doorway facing south. A house with a west facing doorway would face the setting, rather than the rising, sun... with possible poetic allusions.

Variations on a fundamental theme contribute to the subtlety of architecture.

73

INTERLUDE: Korowai tree house; Farnsworth House

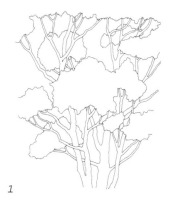

1

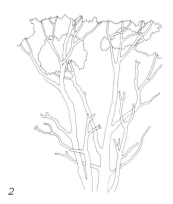

2

3

The Korowai tribe of Western Papua live in houses they build high in the trees. These houses are examples of various kinds of architectural geometry, but especially the geometry of making.

First the architect-builders choose a tree (1) and clear others around to give it space and light. Next they thin some of the upper branches partly to reduce the amount the tree rocks in the wind but primarily to make space for the house amongst the branches (2). Rather than draw a circle of place on the ground the Korowai establish a sphere of place up in the branches of the tree (3).

Some branches are trimmed to provide particular support for the platform that forms the floor of the house (4). This platform is horizontal. It establishes the area - the stage - on which the life of the house will take place. It is made of a grid of straight pieces of timber, laid as regularly as possible, one layer at right angles on top of the other. A ladder, with widely spaced rungs, links the platform back to the ground.

A framework of walls and roof, pitched to shed the rain, is built on the platform (5). These components are constructed of grids of straight pieces of timber too. The walls and roof are clad with leaves to make them water- and wind-proof (6). The floor is laid with unrolled sheets of bark, roughly rectangular.

The first thing when the house is finished is to light a fire (!) at the centre of the floor, establishing its occupation and making it a home. The Korowai tree house is a composition of geometries working together: the circle (or sphere) of place, with the hearth at the centre; the anthropometry of the ladder and the dimensions of the house; and principally, the geometry of making in the regular framework of straight timbers which contrasts with the irregularity of the tree's branches.

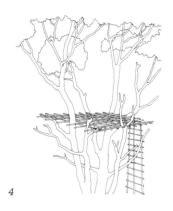

4

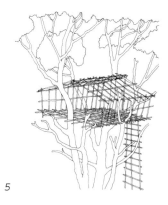

5

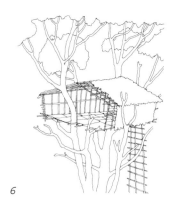

6

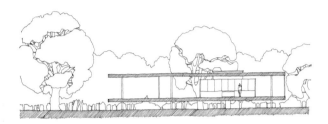

section

The geometry of making does not only condition
buildings built in traditional ways from timber,
stone and brick. It exerts an equally powerful
'gravitational pull' in relation to building
in materials such as rolled steel and plate
glass. Mies van der Rohe's Farnsworth House is
a case in point. In its design the geometry of
making is rigorously applied. The result is
an orthogonal (rectangular) building with the
accommodation sandwiched between two parallel
planes, floor and roof. The columns holding
these two planes apart are evenly spaced,
supporting long beams that stretch the length
of the house. Between these span the floor and
roof beams, regularly spaced to support the
sub-structure (1). The dimensions of the floor,
and the adjacent outdoor platform, fit an exact
number of stone (travertine) flooring slabs (2).

(The Farnsworth House is one of the buildings
analysed in Twenty Buildings Every Architect
Should Understand.)

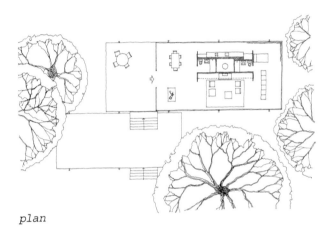

plan

1

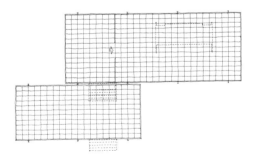

2

IN YOUR NOTEBOOK...

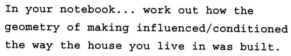

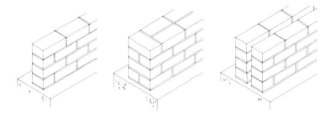

Our house has walls of different thicknesses, all built of the same brick. Internal walls are one brick thick. Some external walls are two bricks thick. Others, facing the prevailing weather, have two skins of brickwork with a 2" (51mm) cavity between.

In your notebook... work out how the geometry of making influenced/conditioned the way the house you live in was built.

Above is my house; it was built about a hundred years ago. Drawings 4 and 2 on the following page show the ground (US first) and first (US second) floors. To the original house we added the single storey part (shown only in outline on the upper floor plan, 2).

Though the walls are covered externally with a layer of cement render and internally by plaster I know they are built of fired clay bricks, slightly bigger than used in the UK today, nominally 3" high x 4½" wide x 9" long (76mm x 114mm x 229mm). The geometry of the brick conditions the geometry of the walls. The basic principle is that these standard-sized bricks are laid in even courses starting on an even horizontal foundation of concrete poured into a trench dug in the ground and allowed to set hard. Mortar joints, both horizontal and vertical, are evenly ½" wide.

Whole books have been written on the subtleties of building brick walls - there is no space to repeat them here - but this basic principle suggests it is sensible (though not obligatory) to: build brick walls vertical, perpendicular to

the force of gravity and the horizontal foundation; make openings rectangular and horizontal/vertical; make lengths of wall a whole number of half bricks (not always possible); and make the heights of walls, and window sills and their heads, a whole number of courses above the foundation (this is not always possible either).

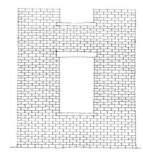

Here, to illustrate, is a portion of wall from my house stripped of its cement render. There are six whole bricks from the corner of the wall to the window. The window is five whole bricks wide and twenty one high. Then there are another six whole bricks to the other corner. The window sill is (in the drawing) twelve bricks above the concrete foundation (there may be more but I am uncertain of the depth of the foundation below the surface of the ground). There are also twelve brick

It is usual to draw upper floor plans directly above lower floor plans, so that they may be read intuitively. In the plans of my house you can see that the upper floor plan is not exactly congruent with the lower. At one point (a) a brick wall upstairs has no wall below, so it has to be supported on a steel beam (not shown). Another upstairs wall (b) is just supported on the timber floor, but it is light, being made not of bricks but of compressed straw boards. Generally the weight of upstairs walls should be taken right down to the ground through corresponding walls beneath.

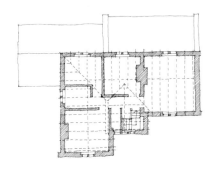

1

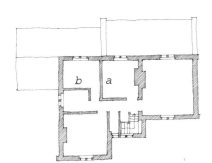

2

courses between the head of the downstairs window and the sill of the upstairs window, though two of these are occupied by the lintel that supports the wall directly above the window. The whole is an exercise in harmonizing the size of the wall and its openings with the size of the standard brick. This is part of the geometry of making.

The floors and roofs of my house are also conditioned by the geometry of making. You can see from the drawings that the plan is orthogonal, composed of rectangles with parallel opposite walls. This not only accords with the rectangular geometry of the bricks but also makes it easier to build the intermediate floor and roof. Drawing 3 shows the direction of the evenly spaced floor joists over the downstairs of the original house and the rafters in the roofs over our additions. (The wider spaced rafters are in the glass roof of a conservatory or sun room.) As in the Welsh House on page 71 the floorboards run at right angles to these joists; and ceiling boards are fixed to their underside.

Drawing 1 shows the parallel rafters and ridges of the roof of the original house. Battens (not shown) onto which the roof slates are fixed run parallel to each other and at right angles to these rafters.

The slates are laid to their own geometry. They too, like the bricks, are of a standard size, 14" x 7" (356mm x 178mm).

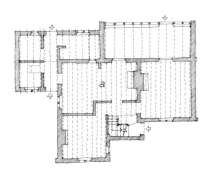

3

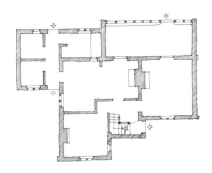

4

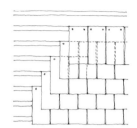

1

They are laid as shown in the drawing
alongside (1). Because they are rectangular
they fit neatly next to each other in rows
(also called courses). But the bottom edge
of each slate must overlap two courses
beneath, so that water will not leak
through the joints.

Doors and windows are conditioned by the
geometry of making too (2 - 3). They fit
into the rectangular, brick sized, openings
left in the walls. They are constructed
from straight pieces of timber, rectangular
in section (4, though windows would not
be made like this today). The small panes
are all the same size so that the glass
can be cut to a standard size. Rectangular
windows, like doors, are easier to open and
close. The lower windows in the drawing (3)
have hinges down one side. The upper are
hinged at the top. The geometry of making
conditions the ways components in buildings
are able to be moved as well as the ways in
which they are made.

There are other components in the
house that follow the geometry of making.
Some walls and floors are finished with
rectangular clay tiles. Some of the floors
downstairs have parquet - wood blocks, 9"
x 2¾" (229mm x 70mm) - laid in a regular
herringbone pattern (5). Blocks are cut
where they meet the walls.

Now measure where you live and draw the
ways the geometry of making has conditioned
its form.

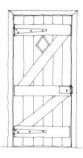

2

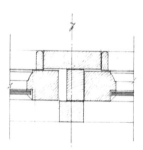

3

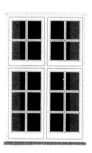

4

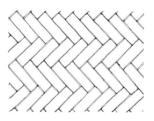

5

INTERLUDE: a classic form, with innumerable variations and extensions

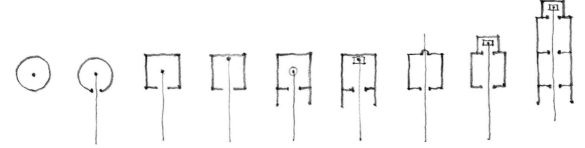

Through an exploratory process that began with the circle of place with its centre (focus), and has included the doorway axis, social geometry and the geometry of making, we have reached one of the classic forms of architecture. This classic form is found in buildings all around the world in just about every human culture. It has many variations (some of which are shown above, in the form of 'parti' sketches) but its essential ingredients are an enclosed space with a doorway, the axis of which indicates the place of a focus. That focus might be a hearth, a person, an effigy (of a god), an altar, or even another doorway. The focus can be internal, external or both at the same time. The doorway's threshold defines a line of transition from outside to in and vice versa.

The doorway axis is one that can be occupied and travelled along by the person. In this way, the classic form can be seen to be an instrument of linkage (between the person and the focus of attention) and also a route of aspiration, perhaps through a series of stages punctuated by doorways (their thresholds).

Here are three of innumerable examples: 1. the Greek temple; 2. the Islamic (Turkish) mosque; 3. the Christian church. Each orients the person to: 1. the effigy of a god, and that to the rising sun; 2. the direction of Mecca (the centre of faith) indicated by the mihrab doorway in the qibla wall; and 3. the altar and the east (the direction of the rising sun).

Notice how there is a reminder of the original circle of place in the form of the semicircular dome over the mosque, and the semicircular apse behind the church's high altar.

The idea of the 'inner sanctum' is a great deal older than any of these three examples. La Bajoulière (4), that dolmen in the Loire valley in France, is over 5000 years old. Built of huge stones (megaliths), it has a covered porch leading into a 'nave' from which leads a further doorway into the mysterious inner room.

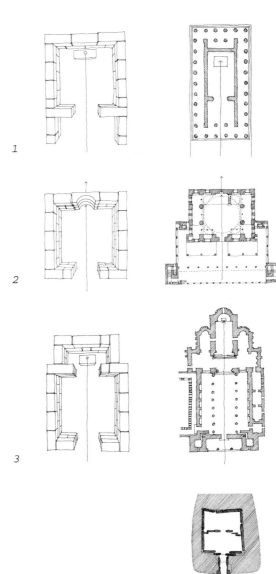

1

2

3

4

EXERCISE 7e. Spanning greater distances.

Within the limitations of children's building blocks it is difficult to explore the more sophisticated ways spaces may be spanned if the materials available are not long or strong enough to span them in one go. You can however experiment. Here are three fundamentally different ways; each has its historical precedents. All may, to some extent, be modelled using your blocks.

Corbelling. The principle of this structure can be used over circular, square or oval spaces that are too large to be spanned in one go. Here it is used to put a roof over a square space (*1*). First one has to span the doorway. If it is too wide for a single lintel, you can first narrow the span in steps (*2*); these steps must be gradual. This is the principle of corbelling. It can be applied to the roof as a whole. The open space is reduced by spanning across the corners (*3*). This process is repeated until the space is covered completely (*4-6*). Using small or irregular stones, this process has to be even more gradual than with your building blocks. It usually results in a conical dome. Corbelling has been used to span some large spaces, as in the Treasury of Atreus at Mycenae, Greece (above), which spans nearly 15 metres (50′).

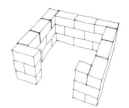
1

2

3

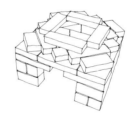
4

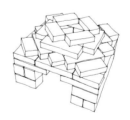
5

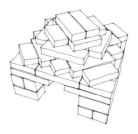
6

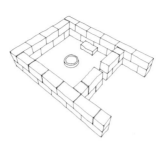

1

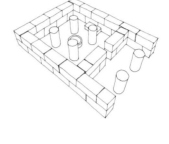

2

Many other examples of corbelling can be found from the ancient, prehistoric and pre-industrial world.

Columns and beams. Another way of spanning larger spaces is by introducing intermediate columns (1-2). This reduces spans to suit the lengths and strengths of material available (3). Secondary structure, and roof or floor coverings, can then be constructed on this primary structure of columns and beams.

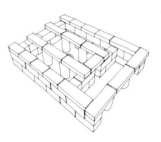

This structure has been used since ancient Egypt and before. It is also the principle of the Mycenaean *megaron* (above) in which four columns reduce spans whilst also allowing the hearth to retain its central position.

3

So long as the columns are stable (will not fall over) the peripheral wall is not needed, allowing structured but open spaces amongst the columns. This is the principle behind Le Corbusier's 'Dom-Ino' idea (1918, below) which was very influential in twentieth century architecture. Such open columned spaces are common in reinforced concrete and steel framed structures.

4

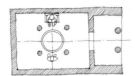

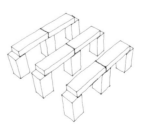

5

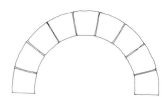

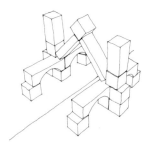

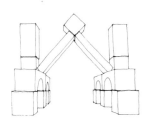

1

2

Arch. It is not possible to build a typical arch with children's building blocks without cutting them to the appropriate shapes. But you can build a very simple arch (*1-2*), composed of just two 'stones' (voussoirs) with a 'key-stone'. You will find that the towers at each side (buttresses) are needed to stop the arch spreading and collapsing. Though this simple arch is not as sophisticated as the structure of a vaulted cathedral, it does demonstrate the principle on which it is based (*3*, this one has a timber structure supporting a weatherproof roof above the stone arches and vaulting). Cathedral arches and vaults are constructed of many smaller pieces of stone cut precisely to shape. Notice in the drawing how this cathedral also has those buttresses that prevent the arch from spreading and collapsing.

3

The challenges and opportunities of structural design are seductive. Much architecture through history – from ancient to recent times – is a demonstration of structural prowess. But it is worth remembering that architecture is, in the first place, concerned with framing people and their activities. The space spanned by a succession of arches with vaulting between, in the grandest cathedral, frames the axial relationship between the worshipper and the altar (*4-5*).

4

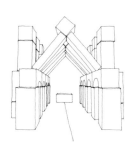

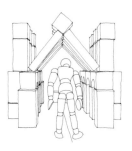

5

IN YOUR NOTEBOOK...

1

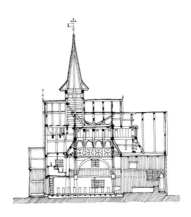

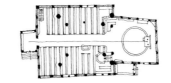

2

**In your notebook... find and draw examples
of structural geometries.** In the preceding
exercise, it has not been possible to model
all the possible variations of structural
geometry found in buildings ancient and
recent; using children's blocks is too
restricting. Study buildings you visit,
and others you see in publications, to
understand their structural order. Do not
forget to study also the relationships they
illustrate between structural order and
spatial organisation, as discussed in the
chapter 'Space and Structure' in *Analysing
Architecture*.

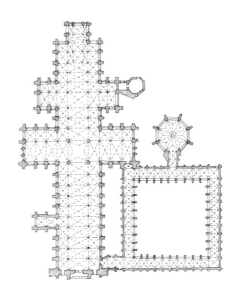

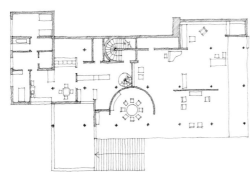

4

3

1. *Slate house in Wales. The geometry of making
structure conditions form even if the materials
used are irregular.*

2. *Norwegian Stave church. The geometry of
structure can be the geometry of space too. The
circle of place is remembered in front of the
altar.*

3. *Salisbury Cathedral. The different geometries
of structure frame different activities:
processing to the altar; discussion in the
octagonal chapter house; perambulating in the
square cloister.*

4. *Tugendhat House (Mies van der Rohe, 1931).
There may be more subtle relationships between
structural geometry and spatial organisation.*

INTERLUDE: a conflict in the geometry of making (for a reason) – Asplund's Woodland Chapel (again)

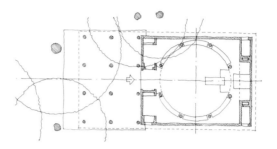

plan

Asplund's Woodland Chapel has been the subject of a previous Interlude (page 35). Now we can look it again and observe one way in which its architect, whilst generally submitting to the geometry of making, found himself faced with a conflict in geometries. He resolved these in the way that he did for particular poetic reasons.

Generally the framework of the chapel's roof has the three dimensional geometry one would expect in a traditional timber roof structure. But just as Asplund inserts the circle of place – in the form of the circle of columns – into the rectangle of the plan, so he wants to form a dome within the roof. His symbolism is that of the sky. And light enters to reflect off its smooth white surface from a roof light at the ridge.

The spherical geometry of the dome does not fit into the framework of the roof, so Asplund has to design for it its own geometry. And to find it place (rather like the Korowai tribes people cutting out branches high in their tree to find place for their new house) Asplund cuts out part of the timber roof structure.

The discipline/authority of the roof structure's geometry of making is contravened for what Asplund clearly saw as a higher purpose – the poetic symbolism of the place he designed for the funerals of children. Outside his chapel appears like a cottage with a simple hipped roof. Inside it is an ancient stone circle under the dome of an artificial sky. The geometries of each do not match. There has to be compromise (on the part of the traditional timber roof structure). One might think of Asplund's device as 'theatrical', in the sense that he contrives an artificial scene within the container of the chapel's external form. As often the case with theatrical scenes, they may (need) not obey the same pragmatic geometries as ordinary buildings.

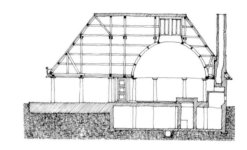

long section

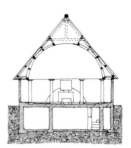

cross section

AN OBSERVATION: attitudes to the geometry of making

The geometry of making does not impinge on the form of places identified merely by choice and occupation (in the landscape for example). Transforming the canopy of a tree into a shelter just by sitting under it, or the slope of a sand dune into a seat by sitting on it, or a cave into a house by living in it, does not invoke the geometry of making. But as soon as an architect intervenes physically, changes the world by making something - even if slightly - then the influence of the geometry of making comes into play.

The architect who rings the trunk of a tree with a bench has to find a way of making a circle (or perhaps an octagon, hexagon, pentagon...) by joining together straight pieces of timber. The architect who walls up the mouth of his cave has to weave wattle from sticks or build stones

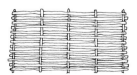

upon each other taking into account the geometry of making suited to the materials available and fitting that geometry into the irregular mouth of the cave.

Even the architect who inscribes a circle about herself in the sand with a stick invokes the geometry of making with the radius of her turn and the point of the stick.

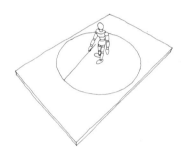

Joining, weaving, building, turning... all invoke the geometry of making.

And as soon as you - the architect - begin to intervene physically, to change the world by making (rather than just inhabiting) a place, then what you do, whether as designer (mind) or as designer and builder (maker), is informed by what you want to achieve and by your attitude to the geometry of making.

At first, you might be content to lash together some rudimentary construction using whatever you have to hand. You might, for example, make your seat on the sand dune roughly from found pieces of driftwood. But this is one of various attitudes one might have to the geometry of making. You might act on the basis that the geometry of making is...

• merely a condition of building, a factor that has to be taken into account but no more than necessary to construct what might be judged a 'good enough' structure;

• something analogous to the genetic programme of building, a conditioning authority that should be followed in pursuit of constructed form that is perfectly, maybe organically, integrated;

• a human (which some consider morally questionable) imposition on the natural shapes of materials, and therefore to be resisted;

• an arena for the display of ingenuity, invention, skill, daring, prowess...;

• mundane, boring, earthbound... a factor to be transcended.

Each attitude to the geometry of making is associated with its own convictions and asserts its own virtues. But there is no one right attitude to the geometry of making. The result of this plurality is the promiscuity of architecture; it is part of the reason why a thatched cottage is different from a rococo church, a classical temple different from what has been termed 'blobitecture'. The geometry of making is a locus of wordless philosophy. Attitudes to it stretch along a dimension from submission and obedience to conceit and transcendence.

Since ancient times people have exercised and celebrated their capacity to achieve constructions that surpass the rudimentary, the 'good enough'. The further their achievements surpass what is presumed to be possible the better they fulfil their aspirations.

If you managed to perch a ten ton slab of rock on the tips of three others stood upright you too would feel some pride in your human capacity to achieve.

The mind–nature dialectic

In architecture, the geometry of making is alternatively seen as either an arena for the exercise of the mind's capacity to do (ingenuity, invention...) or as a rein (an inconvenient and resented restriction) on its aspirations. The geometry of making is a field of play on which the designing mind meets nature. Left to itself, nature prevails by the action of its implacable mindless properties, processes, forces. The mind that sets itself to do something finds itself in a contest with nature; its attempts at action conditioned by those properties, processes, forces. Put simply, the mind has three choices: to submit; to strive to overcome; or to work to find some harmony between its aspirations and the conditions imposed by nature.

Examples of different attitudes

The burial chamber of Maes Howe (above, Orkney) was built around 2600 BCE. It is classified as 'prehistoric', 'primitive', 'rudimentary'. Nevertheless it illustrates the ingenuity of the mind that conceived it. It has a clear geometry of making resulting from an interplay between the designing mind (its intention) and the possibilities of the materials available. The mind (the architect) has determined on a rectangular chamber with a corbelled roof, achieved with flat slabs of stone laid in fairly regular courses. Maes Howe was conceived by a mind sensitive to the character and possibilities of the material available and the physical strength and skill of the people who built it. It illustrates a harmonious interplay

between the mind (its will and ingenuity) and nature (the character of the material available).

From the rectangular ceiling panels to the tatami mats on the floor, the rectangular rooms and the framed windows and shoji screens, the design of a traditional Japanese house (above) is governed by the geometry of making brought to a high level of discipline and perfection. As a counterpoint, some elements are allowed to retain their irregular natural form or patterning of natural grain and texture. In the picture a curving branch is used as the corner of a cubicle, forming half the frame of an oval window. The result is an intriguing interplay between natural form and the tendency to the rectangular of the geometry of making. This has been done not through necessity but by selection (of a particular branch the form of which prompts and satisfies the designing mind's vision) and deliberate intention. This example illustrates the designing mind's capacity

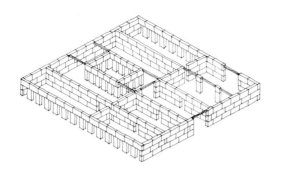

The Wine Store at the Winery in Vauvert, France by Gilles Peraudin (1998, left) is a rare contemporary example of a building built simply according to the geometry of making. The building is made mainly of standard sized stone blocks (1050 x 2600 x 520 mm) cut orthogonally at the quarry. Though much bigger and heavier, they are put together just like the blocks on your board. Their rectangular geometry is in harmony with the rectangular plan (which is also axial). The roof structure is timber beams spanning between the parallel walls.

to use the geometry of making as an arena for contemplating a poetic relationship between itself, the forms of natural things such as trees, stones, water, light..., contrasting with the tendency of built form to the rectangular. The branch stands as a representative of natural irregularity set (maybe imprisoned) amongst other materials (natural too) that have been 'de-natured' by sawing, planing, squaring, smoothing, polishing. The result is aesthetically pleasing and philosophically engaging.

Sometimes the geometry of making is presented as the touchstone of frugality, austerity, piety, adherence to 'God's law'.

When Dom Hans van der Laan designed the Abbey of St Benedict at Vaals in the Netherlands (above, in the 1960s), everything – the plan, the section, the shapes of the walls and the openings in them, steps... – was subjected to the discipline of the regular rectangular geometry of the brick.

The same attitude is apparent in the cells designed for Louis Kahn's unbuilt (also 1960s) project for a Dominican Motherhouse near Philadelphia.

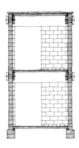

All is disciplined by the geometry – the rectangularity and dimensions – of the blocks from which the walls were to be built. This attitude is pragmatic – it suggests the attractive idea of 'building simply' – but it too is philosophical. It implies rigour, self-control, an avoidance (a distaste for) showiness, for unnecessary ornamentation. The discipline of the brick (the geometry of making) is seen as a metaphorical equivalent of the discipline of the life of the nun or monk.

In sixteenth century Istanbul, the Sultan's architect Sinan celebrated religious faith and conviction with audacious domes – opposite top is the Süleymaniye mosque, based on the Haghia Sophia built some twelve hundred years earlier – that stretched the geometry of making as far as (if not beyond where) his courage and belief in the dependability

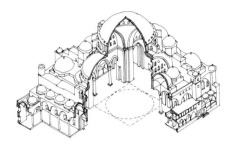

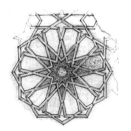

of structural integrity would allow. In this building, religious faith is not expressed by self-denial, simplicity and adherence to the restrictive discipline of the geometry of a simple element such as a brick. It celebrates the audacity and ingenuity of the designing mind which subjects material to its will. But that mind also takes into account and uses (exploits) the character of the material available (stone) and the force of gravity (which is the main 'glue' that holds the shaped stones together in the forms of the domes). Here the ingenuity and courage of the mind is not seen as in potential conflict with the will of Allah (expressed through nature) but as an instrument of it. The Süleymaniye celebrates the mind (and the physical prowess) of the human being as an instrument of God's will. And this is expressed through the geometry of making.

The inventiveness and ingenuity of the mind may be celebrated without reference to a supernatural authority or creator. In the roof over the Great Court of the

British Museum in London (below left), Norman Foster stretched the geometry of making in a different way from Sinan in the Süleymaniye. He did so literally, by taking a regular mesh (that would frame the glazed panels) and morphing it (with the help of a computer program) to reconcile the geometric disparity between the rectangular perimeter of the court and the circular library at its centre.

Stretching the geometry of making requires ingenuity, effort and the dedication of substantial resources of money, labour, time... To build simply according to the geometry of making may be seen as a frugal way of doing things. To build in grand, complex, audacious ways can be seen as an expression of worship, faith, sacrifice; it can also be an expression of status, grandiosity, self-importance on the part of the person or institution that commits those resources.

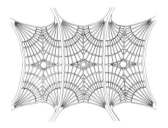

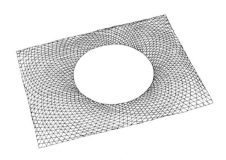

The fan-vaulted ceiling of King's College Chapel in Cambridge (above) is an intricate example of how far the geometry

of making can be stretched. Even though it is pragmatically redundant – there is an unseen simple timber-structured roof above it to keep out the weather (above) – in its ingenuity, beauty and commitment of resources, it is an expression of the College's wealth, status, taste, aspirations and connections.

Some buildings manifest, on purpose, a disregard for the geometry of making; their architects refuse to accept that it might hold authority over what they do. In some cases architects and their patrons have felt that the geometry of making should be considered not so much as a condition of building to be followed, nor as an ingredient of a poetic interplay between regularity and natural form, nor stretched as far as (or further than) ingenuity may achieve... but as a condition to be considered mundane, lowly, to be disparaged as unworthy or demeaning and which an architect should strive to transcend, to rise above.

Adhering to the apparent authority of the geometry of making is cheaper, easier, perhaps more sensible. Ignoring it in favour of other shapes is expensive, difficult and risky. It is because of this that ignoring the geometry of making is attractive. It can produce sensational results that defy the spectator's sense of 'sense'. And some patrons (clients) want the sensational rather than sense.

The sensational inspires awe and grabs attention.

Awe and attention can be as important to religion as frugality and simplicity. And the former can be acquired by consigning the geometry of making to obscurity rather than following where it leads.

The Rococo churches built in central Europe in the eighteenth century are examples. Above is a drawing of a typical Rococo pulpit. Though obviously it must hold together and not collapse, nothing about its form adheres to the geometry of making. It is designed to be extravagant, inspiring worshippers with awe at the power and wealth of the church, and 'entertaining' them with sensational shows and dynamic compositions of saints, star bursts and other golden embellishments.

Just as ingenuity has its secular as well as religious manifestations, so too

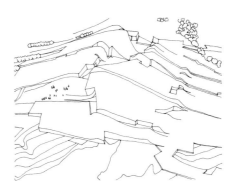

does sensationalism. Producing something sensational is an effective device in advertising.

When Frank Gehry produced the Guggenheim Museum in Bilbao, Spain, in the 1990s it transformed the fortunes of a struggling city by attracting millions of visitors to admire its sensational form.

And that form can be analysed as a product principally of distortion. It is as if a block model had been photographically distorted.

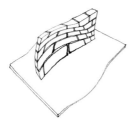

To build the original block model was easy. But to build the distorted version would require a great deal of time both to determine the shape each block should be and to form it.

The curved titanium cladding of the Guggenheim is a distortion of the rectangular geometry of making (which requires a complicated geometry of steel structure to underpin it). It represents a commitment on the part of the city and national Spanish authorities to expend resources in the hope of attracting visitors. Many cities across the world have followed this example; above, is the Centre of Culture in Galicia, designed by Peter Eisenman.

Varying attitudes to the geometry of making contribute to the promiscuity of architectural form. But attention drawn to form in this sense, whether simple and sensible or sensational and risky, can be attention drawn away from the person as ingredient of architecture. The architect of the Guggenheim in Bilbao is not acting as servant, nurse, politician, philosopher... making a considerate frame (physical and abstract) to accommodate the person. He is acting as impresario, showman, gymnast... making a show to impress, to astonish rather than frame the person. From being the main ingredient of architecture, the person is consigned to the role of a spectator.

(See also Exercise 11, Playing with Geometry, on pages 137-152.)

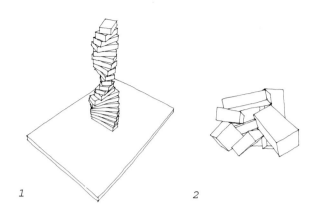

1   2

EXERCISE 7f. Transcending the geometry of making.

It will require time and effort, but if you wish you can attempt to build with your blocks a form that in some way transcends the geometry of making. You can aim for ingenuity or sensationalism.

You might start by seeing what you could do using the blocks as they are: putting them together in more complex or irregular ways (*1* and *2*); trying to build something that looks implausible or impossible (*3*); making a complex shape appear as if it has been carved from or moulded in a single block of material (maybe by plastering over the blocks, *4*); perhaps composing them in forms intended to represent something such as a dog (or is it a camel? *5*); or using specially shaped standard blocks (*6*).

But if you really wish to achieve sensational form then you would have to put time and effort into reshaping the blocks or using other materials that were more mouldable into irregular or curved shapes.

You can see that in these compositions too that attention has moved away from making a frame for inhabitation into a fascination with what might be called 'sculptural form'.

All of these are devices that architects have used to make sensational buildings.

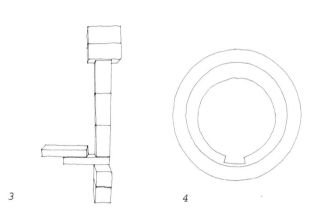

3   4

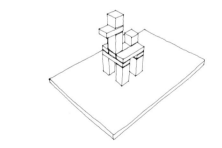

5

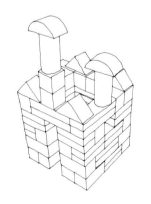

6

IN YOUR NOTEBOOK...

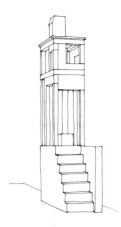

The Architecture Research Unit's 'folly' for Gwangju has three parts: a stepped base; an aedicule containing an altar; and a lantern. On the top is a nesting box for magpies.

In your notebook... find and draw examples that illustrate different attitudes to the geometry of making.

In the second decade of the twenty-first century you can do this by picking up any edition of a contemporary journal on architecture.

As I was writing this the latest copy of the British journal *Building Design* (Friday April 15, 2011) fell through my letter box. On page 4 is an illustration of The Architecture Research Unit's proposal for a 'folly' for the Gwangju Design Biennale to be held in Korea. One photograph shows the concept model which, like the models you have made in these exercise, was built of wooden blocks, except that in this case the blocks are not standard but cut specially. Nevertheless the composition adheres to the rectangular geometry of making. The accompanying article says the final building will be made of concrete, in situ. Its rectangular form will suit the geometry of making the formwork for pouring the concrete too. It seems however that the architects propose indicating joints in the surface of the folly, to suggest not that it is moulded from a single material but composed of a collection of L-shaped panels. At first their attitude to the geometry of making seems simple but with analysis it becomes more subtle and complex, blending apparent honesty of construction with artful deceit.

On page 17 of the same edition of Building Design a very different attitude to the geometry of making is illustrated in Chalibi Architects' design for the Darmstadium in Germany.

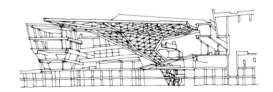

Their attitude is one of distortion made possible by the use of computer based 'building information modelling' (an article on which this building is used to illustrate).

Later in the same edition (on pages 20–24) David Chipperfield's design for the

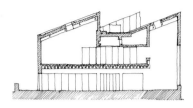

section

new Turner Contemporary Museum in Margate
is shown in photographs and drawings.
In this building the geometry of making
is followed as scrupulously as possible.
This geometry is evident externally in the
regular striations of the framework holding
the glass cladding and glazing panels. But
internally the geometry of this framework
is largely hidden by the finishes to walls
and ceilings, with the constructional grid
evident only in the wall and roof glazing.
Functionally this provides smooth wall
surfaces for hanging art. Architecturally
it dematerialises the fabric suggesting
the interior spaces are carved from a
single substance. The floors too are smooth
polished concrete.

Attitudes to the geometry of making are
subject to argument. Some might argue that
clear expression of honest straightforward
construction, disciplined by the geometry
of making, possesses a quality akin to
moral rectitude and that this influences
its aesthetic appreciation. Others might
argue that construction (the geometry of
making) is something to be transcended in
architecture - i.e. the aim should be to
astonish with form that defies expectation
and even belief. Yet others might argue
that the sort of distortion evident in
the Darmstadium (on the previous page) is
a morally questionable (and expensive)
indulgence. You will have to decide on your
own attitude to the geometry of making.

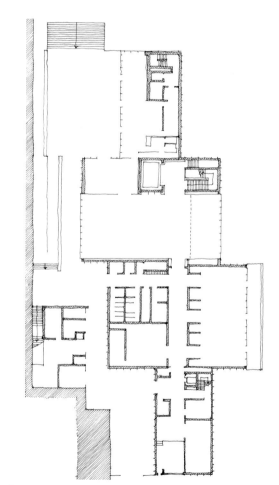

plan

EXERCISE 8: the geometry of planning

The geometry of making, as we have already seen, influences the shapes of rooms and spaces. It suggests that rooms be rectangular, with parallel opposite walls, to make them easier to build. Standard rectangular bricks build most easily into flat, vertical, rectangular walls with regular horizontal courses. They also readily fit right angled corners. Together with the ease of making floors and roofs by spanning regular sized beams between parallel walls, the geometry of making predisposes the architect (who wants to make life easy) to make rooms rectangular.

In this exercise you will begin to look at, and appreciate, how rectangular rooms and spaces also make planning easier. It is easier to build rooms next to each other, sharing party walls, if those rooms are rectangular. It is easier to combine rooms and spaces into plans that are more complex than single rooms, if those rooms and spaces are rectangular rather than irregular. This is the state to which sense tends; though that does not necessarily mean it is always the right (most practical, most interesting, most poetic...) response to a given programme. Other factors may come into play.

EXERCISE 8a. Parallel walls.

A house is a manifestation of the circle of place.

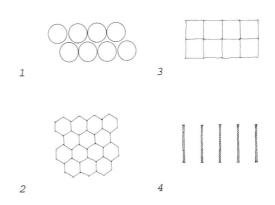

But circles do not tessellate well (1). Redundant gaps are produced. Circular houses cannot share walls easily. Bees solve the problem by morphing circles into hexagons (2). But they access their cells through the 'roof' and, except perhaps in wax, hexagons are not easy to lay out or build. Rectangles tessellate best (3); as in the case of bricks or tiles. It is the same for house plans. Rows of parallel walls can extend indefinitely (4), with a house within each space. Each house shares its walls with its immediate neighbours, and floors and roofs are relatively easy to build.

In Exercise 7c we saw that one of the
basic reasons for the rectangular plan
was that it provided a pair of parallel
walls for the support of floor beams and
roof trusses. Another advantage is that it
allows rooms or houses to be put next to
each other economically (in terms of both
the use of space and construction).

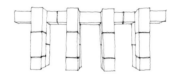

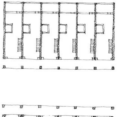

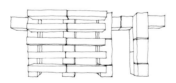

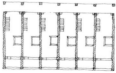

1

Using your blocks, compare the
difficulties of placing circular houses
adjacent to each other with the advantages
of arranging rectangular houses in rows
of parallel walls. You can see that in
parallel wall houses one party wall will
provide half the support needed for the
floors and roofs of two houses (1). Also
there is no wasted space, and rows of
houses can be arranged to face each other
across access streets.

*The parallel wall strategy is the organising
principle of row housing in cities around
the world. These drawings, for example, show
the layout of typical traditional shophouses
found in Malaysia and Singapore. Each house is
accommodated between two parallel walls, with
small interior courtyards for ventilation and
light. The parallel wall arrangement allows many
houses to be arranged side by side, sharing
party walls. Arranged opposite each other,
with a street between, such shophouses are an
efficient way of organising space.*

EXERCISE 8b. Multi-room buildings.

It is also easier to plan houses with many rooms if those rooms are rectangular. With your blocks plan a simple three- or four-room single floor house.

You could subdivide a larger rectangular enclosure of walls...

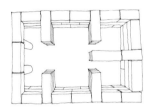

... or compose a less constrained arrangement of rectangular rooms.

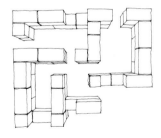

In either case, the process of composition is made easier if the rooms are rectangular.

The rooms of this eighteenth century house in Scotland (The House of Dun by William Adam) are contained and symmetrically arranged within a simple rectangle...

... whereas those in this semi-detached house (below, analysed in terms of the geometry of making on page 76) are composed in an irregular way.

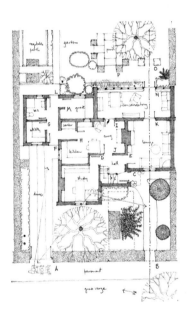

In both, the rectangularity of the rooms serves not only the geometry of making but also the geometry of planning.

Your composition might take an axis
as its datum, with rooms arranged
symmetrically on both sides of a house.

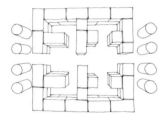

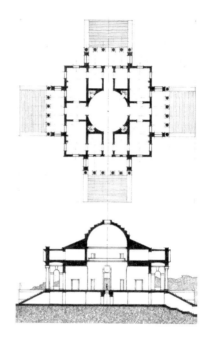

*The rooms of Palladio's Villa Rotonda (sixteenth
century), near Vicenza in Italy, are contained
in concentric squares and arranged symmetrically
around two axes that cross at right angles.*

Again, the process is made easier if all
the component rooms are rectangular and
they fit within a rectangular perimeter.

Consider how a person's experience of a
plan organised symmetrically around an axis
might differ from a plan that is irregular,
even when both are composed of rectangular
rooms.

Consider too the intention and
contribution of the architect in each case.
Is the doorway axis of a simple cell (such
as a hut or Greek temple) the same in its
origin and effects as that of a symmetrical
multi-roomed plan? How much might the
latter be a product of drawing rather than
personal experience of space (i.e. about
the doorway)?

AN OBSERVATION: geometries brought into harmony by the rectangle

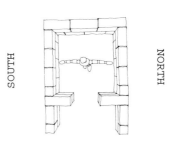

We can now understand the prevalence of rectangular buildings across the world. The rectangle is in accord with geometries relevant to architecture and can bring them into a harmonious relationship.

The rectangle is in accord with:
- the geometry of the person: front, back, right and left;
- the geometry of the world: north, south, east and west;
- the doorway axis; establishing a dynamic line of sight and of passage culminating in a focus.
- the geometry of making; it is easy and sensible to span between its parallel sides;
- the geometry of furniture, itself often governed by the geometry of making;
- social geometries: people sitting around a table or facing a speaker;
- the geometry of planning.

Because it brings various geometries into harmony, the rectangle has been used in architecture since ancient times. It is as amenable today as it was then. The rectangle is the governing principle underlying buildings as diverse as:

1. a small open mud house in Kerala, India (timeless);

2. part of the Palace of Knossos on the island of Crete (c.1500 BCE);

3. an English cathedral (Lincoln, twelfth-fourteenth centuries CE);

4. the Thermal Baths, by Peter Zumthor, in Vals, Switzerland (1996).

Many other examples could have been used. There are too many – the rectangle is so common – that there is no point in trying to collect them in your notebook. (But it does explain why that squared piece of paper is so useful.)

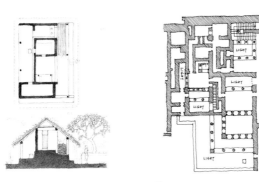
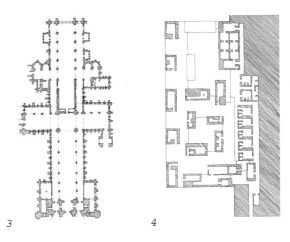

1   2   3   4

INTERLUDE: modifying the rectangular geometry of planning

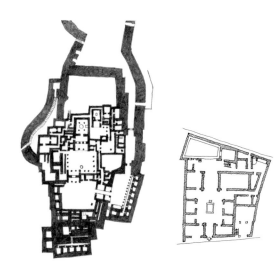

For the reasons stated in the preceding 'Observation', it might be said that the rectangle is the norm in planning buildings; it is, in effect, the 'default setting' for architecture. Deviating from this default setting is one of the great themes of architecture through the ages. Just as music that obediently follows a major key can be tedious so too may architecture that adheres rigidly to the orthogonal. Interest may come from interplay and conflict rather than predictable resolution.

There are various ways of, and reasons for, modifying the default setting of the rectangular. These might be characterised under the headings 'Responsive' and 'Wilful'. (Neither heading is intended here to imply any moral or value judgement, though sometimes they have been and continue to be associated with ideological battles.) These headings are linked to the attitudinal dimensions discussed in Analysing Architecture under the chapter title 'Temples and Cottages'. 'Responsive' reasons for modifying the rectangular are those that derive from responding to conditions. 'Wilful' reasons are those that derive from the architect's desire to impose an extraneous idea. It is not always easy to unravel one from the other. It is always a matter of the (designing) mind's relationship with the world in which it intervenes (through architecture). The dimensions that stretch between the responsive and the wilful have affected architecture through all history.

The Mycenaean builders of the Palace of Tyrins (above left, c.1400 BCE) applied the rectangular geometries of making and planning across the usable area of a hilltop in what is now the Peloponnese in modern Greece. In one special place – the megaron, the heart of the palace – they also employed the power of the doorway axis. But when they met the edges of that usable plateau, where the slopes became too steep, those rectangular geometries gave way to accommodate the irregularities of the land.

Some of the Roman houses in Pompeii (above right) had to fit their regular geometry into irregular sites. The irregularities were hidden away in less important rooms while the main spaces were arranged about an axis originating with the doorway.

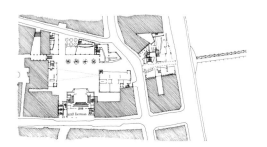

In the early 1990s a consortium of architects called Group '91 designed a series of interventions to regenerate the Temple Bar district of Dublin. Part of this regeneration created a new public space called 'Meeting House Square' (left). It is rectangular. But where its bounding buildings meet the edges of their sites or hit up against irregular existing buildings, their geometries of making and planning have to give way.

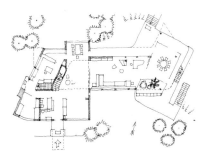

The Hôtel de Beauvais in Paris was designed by Antoine le Pautre in the seventeenth century. Like the Pompeii house opposite, it occupies what was an irregular site between rue François-Miron and rue de Jouy. But by projecting an axis perpendicular to the mid point of the elevation to rue François-Miron, le Pautre conspired to make the visitor feel they were entering a formally symmetrical building. The irregularities of the site are hidden away in less important rooms.

By contrast, Hans Scharoun distorted the geometries of making and planning in the Schminke House (1933) to relate its spaces to the sun and to views. (See Case Study 6 in Analysing Architecture.)

The early nineteenth century British architect John Soane packed many axially symmetrical spaces into the irregular site of the Bank of England in London.

Hugo Häring, like Scharoun in some of his later 1930s houses, designed this unbuilt house (1946) with disregard for the geometries of making and planning. Only in the bedrooms is there some semblance of fitting the rooms to the rectangular beds. His aim, like that of Scharoun, might be said to free the person from the 'tyranny' of the rectangle and axis.

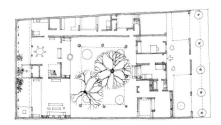

Something similar, though not so grand, happens in Geoffrey Bawa's design for a house in Colombo, Sri Lanka (1962). The narrowing of the site is hidden in the smaller rooms along the right hand edge of the house. All other spaces are orthogonal.

The geometry of Alvar Aalto's Säynätsalo Town Hall (1951) is broken to respond to the line of approach and to avoid any sense of a formal axial entrance.

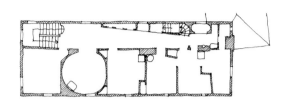

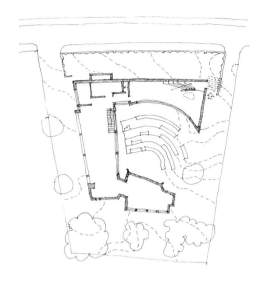

In his Villa Snellman (1918) the Swedish
architect Erik Gunnar Asplund (who also designed
the Woodland Chapel - see pages 35 and 84 -
around the same time) distorted the geometries
of making and planning to create visual effects.
This is the upstairs plan. The landing narrows
to exaggerate perspective; from the top of the
stairs the landing appears much longer than it
is and from the bathroom door much shorter. One
room, off the landing, has its corners rounded
with timber panelling to make it more womb-like.
The rectangularity of other rooms is distorted
too. Most of the odd, 'left-over', spaces are
made into cupboards.

Aalto's distortion of geometries in his studio
in Helsinki is partly a response to the wedge
shaped site but it also creates an external room
like an amphitheatre, complete with rudimentary
tiers of seating in the grass oriented towards a
wall that could be used for screening movies.

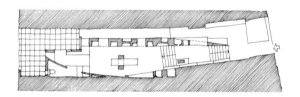

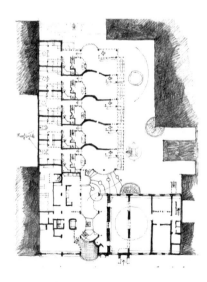

When David Chipperfield designed the Wilson and
Gough Gallery in 1989 he was, like le Pautre
(Hôtel de Beauvais, previous page), presented
with an irregular site. Rather than giving the
irregular space an axis and symmetry he ordered
and organised it with a straight wall. In
counterpoint with the irregularity of the site
this produces different spaces. The design is
an exercise in the interplay of regularity and
irregularity.

Aldo van Eyck gave each of the residential
apartments at the back of the Mothers' House
in Amsterdam (1978) an individual character by
distorting their party walls to make curved
spaces.

**Notice that in all the above examples deviation
from the geometries of making and planning are
not merely graphic exercises. They are all
either responses to (irregular) conditions or
aim to affect the experience of the person. In
some the aim is to persuade the person that,
despite the irregularity of the site, they are
in a regular, ordered, axial place. In others
the aim is to free the person from the axial and
the rectangular and offer different sorts of
spatial experience.**

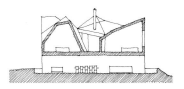

section

While writing these Exercises on the geometries of making and planning, in March 2011, I thumbed through the magazine Architecture Today *(February 2011). There was an article on recent house designs in the UK. The two houses illustrated here demonstrate a contemporary vogue for playing with the geometries of making and planning, their distortion and the different relationship with space that may result.*

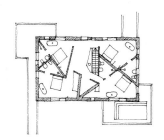

upper floor

upper level

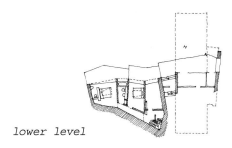

lower level

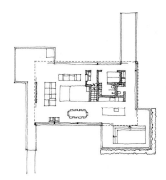

lower floor

Ty Hedfan (Flying, Floating, Hovering House, by Featherstone Young) in mid-Wales, is in two parts. The main part, on two upper levels, is orthogonal while the guest part (built into the ground) to the left in the plans above, is irregular. But even in the orthogonal part there are areas that deviate from the geometry of making.

The Dune House, in Thorpeness, Suffolk (by Jarmond/Vigsnæs Architects), is on two floors. The lower floor is reminiscent of Mies van der Rohe's Farnsworth House (see page 75 and Twenty Buildings Every Architect Should Understand): orthogonal, glass walls all around and with a solid core containing accommodation not to be seen. The upper floor, though contained within a rectangle, is irregular. There are four bedrooms, each containing a bed and a bath, with en suite shower rooms. The upper floor is irregular in section too (top).

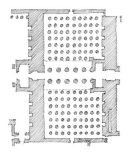
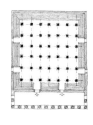

1

EXERCISE 8c. Columned spaces/ the free plan.

In Exercise 7e you explored ways of spanning larger spaces. One of these was to insert intermediate columns within the space to support the roof or floor structure above. Columned spaces have been built since ancient times. Above left is the plan of the hypostyle hall of the Temple of Ammon in Karnak, Egypt, which dates from around 1400BCE. Above right is the Telesterion at Eleusis in Greece (sixth century BCE). These spaces retained their perimeter walls. Their structure was based on the idea that beams could span between relatively closely spaced columns (1). In the twentieth century, when stronger and more integrated structural materials than stone became available architects began makings spaces unbounded by solid perimeter walls. Le Corbusier's 1918 idea of the Dom-Ino House form (2) was a clear and influential expression of this simple but revolutionary architectural idea.

You can explore the ramifications of this revolutionary idea with your building blocks. The circle of place from which all architecture begins is overlaid by a rectangular grid, related to the spanning capabilities of available materials, which determines the positions of the columns (3). This produces a forest of columns, which in ancient times was associated

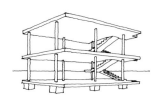

2

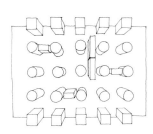

3

4

with mystery. The columns cope with the structure of the roof and the space can be subdivided using partitions that do not carry any structural load (4). The result is an interplay between the columns and the partitions that adds to the language of architecture and its possibilities.

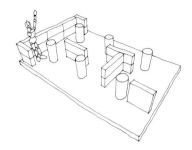

It enables the architect to make spaces that are different in character from those bounded by load-bearing perimeter walls.

The strength and integrity (the ability to make strong joints) of modern materials – reinforced concrete and steel – made larger spans possible, with larger spaces between slimmer columns.

the roof is supported by the columns your partition walls are free to be positioned independently of the columns. They may be under the roof or, equally, not.

Compare this kind of space (above) with that of the 'classic form' identified on page 79. It is not isolated from the outside world. It has no doorway, and hence

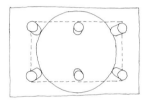

1   *2*   *3*

Start with your circle of place drawn on your board (*1*). Arrange columns to support a notional roof over the circle; due to the geometry of making this has the effect of making the circle rectangular (*2*). Arrange some partition walls independent of this columned structure (*3*). Notice that because

has no doorway axis. It is a space without a single dynamic direction or focus. It is a space within which to wander.

This spatial idea underlies one of the seminal buildings of the twentieth century: Mies van der Rohe's Barcelona Pavilion, 1929. (See *Twenty Buildings*...)

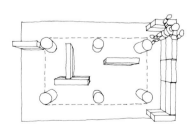

4

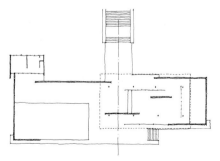

5

IN YOUR NOTEBOOK...

In your notebook... find and draw examples of the 'free' plan, where supporting floors and roofs with (reinforced concrete or steel) columns frees walls of their load-bearing role and produces open rather than enclosed spaces.

You could start with two of the seminal buildings from around 1930 that introduced this new spatial idea to architecture: Mies van der Rohe's Barcelona Pavilion (already mentioned) and Le Corbusier's Villa Savoye. (Both are included as case studies in *Twenty Buildings Every Architect Should Understand*.)

The Barcelona Pavilion notionally begins with eight slim steel columns supporting a flat roof plane (dotted) over a stone podium. This frees the walls to be positioned on the podium, both under and outside the roof. Though Mies seems to have drawn upon the ancient Greek megaron or temple as the basis for his architecture, he breaks open the enclosed cell and creates a simple labyrinth rather than an axially symmetrical plan generated by a doorway and focus. This is a building in which to wander rather than follow a clear direction.

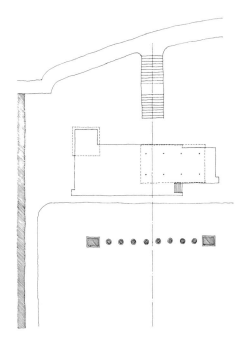 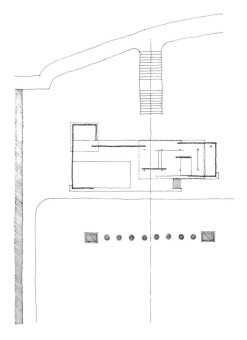

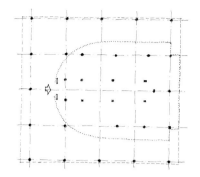

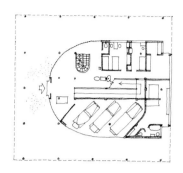

The walls of Le Corbusier's Villa Savoye (this is the ground floor) are independent of the load-bearing structural concrete columns. The doorway (arrowed) is on the central axis of the gridded plan but as soon as the person enters they are diverted from that axis onto a ramped route that takes them up onto the main living floor. Notice how Le Corbusier lets some columns avoid the strict discipline of the structural grid, e.g. to leave space for the central ramp.

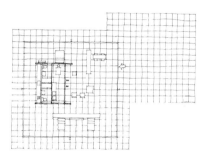

In his unbuilt project for a Fifty by Fifty Foot House, Mies reduced the roof-supporting structure to four slim steel columns situated at the mid point of each of the square's sides.

Some of Aalto's Villa Mairea is built of load-bearing masonry walls. Other parts have structural columns. The Library (bottom right in the drawing) is defined by screens of bookcases which play no structural role.

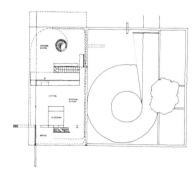

Rem Koolhaas was influenced by Le Corbusier but took some of his ideas to surreal levels. The middle floor of his Maison à Bordeaux seems almost totally without any structure. Koolhaas and his engineer devised a way of making the top floor appear to float over space. (The Maison à Bordeaux is another case study in Twenty Buildings Every Architect Should Understand.)

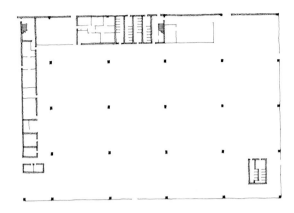

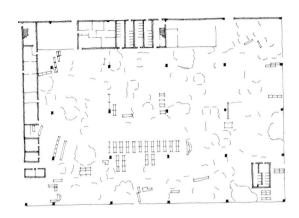

The most common use of the free plan is in office buildings. This is the floor plan of the GEG Mail Order House built in Kamen, West Germany, in the early 1960s. It is a large open space punctuated by structural columns widely spaced on a simple grid. Only lavatories and storerooms, which could not be left open, are in enclosed rooms. The rest is like an open landscape, a beach waiting for inhabitation.

The first elements of inhabitations are screens and other pieces of furniture such as filing cabinets and clothes racks that are used to define space. These act like the windbreaks people sometime erect on the beach to define their own territories. They may be moved in response to varying needs for space.

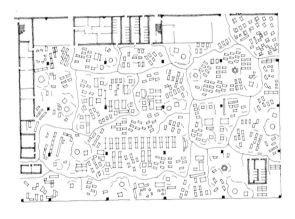

The screens and other pieces of furniture define the territories for the desks of work groups. There are also places with large tables for conferences and discussion. Some territories are allocated for relaxation. Notice how the columns do play a part in how territories are laid out. Notice too that different places have different characters. You choose where you might like to sit to answer the telephone all day.

Pathways thread their ways between the different territories, giving access to each. The resultant layout is like a beach on a busy summer's day. Architecture has created its own formalised artificial landscape. (It was known as bürolandschaft - office landscape.) Social geometries are evident in the layouts of seats, tables, desks. It is also like a nascent urban community growing from small settlements. Nowadays layouts of call centres tend to be more geometrically ordered than this. See the drawing on page 65.

EXERCISE 9: ideal geometry

In the preceding exercises we have explored the influences of various kinds of geometry in architecture. But the one you might have first thought of as 'geometry' comes last. This is the sense of geometry in pure mathematics, the sort of geometry you learnt in school or when you played with a ruler, compasses, protractor... It is the geometry of perfect circles, squares, spheres, cubes... This is an abstract form of geometry distinguishable from the 'existential' forms of geometry (the geometries of being) of the previous exercises (the circle of place; the doorway axis; the geometry of making etc.). To give it its own name, in Analysing Architecture this abstract kind of geometry was termed 'ideal geometry'.

Whereas the natural home of the geometries of being is out in the world – in the characteristics of materials (bricks, blocks, straight lengths of timber), in our bodies – the home of ideal geometry is in the abstract realm of the surface of a flat sheet of paper or the cyberspace of a computer program. The fact that ideal geometry is not quite of this world adds to its mystique, especially for architects. To make a building as a perfect cube, despite there being no pragmatic or experiential reason for doing so, lends it a quality perceived by the mind as transcendent. It seems to give it the authority of the perfect, the ideal.

EXERCISE 9a. A square space.

It is fortuitous that this is Exercise 9. Nine is a square number, 3 x 3. It can be expressed graphically as a square divided into nine equal smaller squares.

In this sense nine is a two-dimensional number. Draw this 3 x 3 square on your board. In laying out this square we shall take into account the centre, the dynamic of architectural space and the geometry of making.

Mark the centre of the board. Outline the 3 x 3 square with the centre of one of its sides at the centre of the board, and use the length of one block as a module.

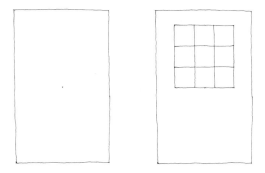

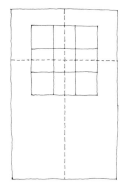

You can see that the square recalls some of the ideas we have encountered previously in these exercises: the generation of its own centre and axes that resonate with the rectangular geometry of the 'world' of the board on which you are going to build.

Now build a wall around this square, just one block high. You might build this wall in three different positions: with the square at its outer face; with the square at its inner face; or with the square at its mid point all the way around. Each would produce a square enclosure; but for this exercise build it with the square at the inner face of the wall.

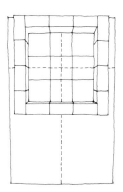

Because you have used the length of one of your blocks as a module, on two of the sides of your square enclosure the joints of the blocks should align with the lines of the smaller squares. Now you have a square enclosed space. But your person would not be able to enter it except by climbing over the wall. So open a doorway. You could place a hearth at the centre too.

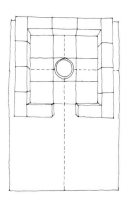

Now we have a building identical in plan to the house we redesigned (from the circular house) in Exercise 7 in response to the geometry of making. But, significantly we have come to it by a different conceptual route. The house in Exercise 7 derived from the circle of place modified to take into account the tendency of the geometry of making to the rectangular. The house we have just built took its plan form from the idea of the ideal geometry of the perfect square. Even though the result is the same, the ideas behind the two houses are different. This conceptual difference becomes more evident and its influence becomes apparent as we try to develop the design.

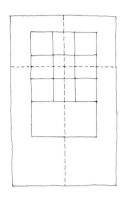 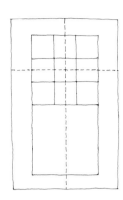

EXERCISE 9b. Extending the square.

In Exercise 7 we added a porch to protect the doorway. According to the geometry of making we just added a couple of blocks to the length of the side walls. But if we are accepting the authority of ideal geometry then we need to determine a different reason for the lengths of the extra portions of side wall needed to make the porch.

There are various ways we might extend the square using ideal geometry.

First we might extend the square by a third, one extra line of smaller squares. This would produce a 3 x 4 rectangle. And since we used the length of a block as a module, it would also be in accord with the geometry of making. We might however judge that it would produce a porch that is not deep enough.

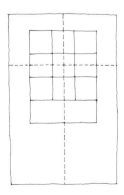

Second, we might extend the large square by a half or even a whole extra square, producing 2 x 3 and 1 x 2 rectangles respectively (above).

But we might think these were rather predictable and dull and look for more interesting ways of using a mathematical method to extend the square.

So, third, we might try taking the diagonal of the square as a radius and describe an arc to cut the extended side.

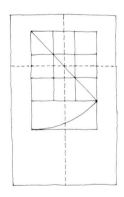 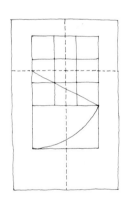

This produces a '√2' rectangle (because the diagonal of a square is the square root of 2).

Or, fourth, we could take the mid point of one side of the square as a centre and again describe an arc from an opposite corner until *it* cuts the extended side.

This produces a 'Golden' rectangle because, as shown on page 162 of the third edition of *Analysing Architecture*, its

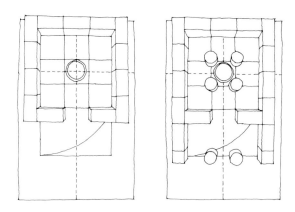

proportions are self-replicating. If you remove the square from a Golden Rectangle, the remaining portion is still a Golden Rectangle.

All these methods of extending the square by means of ideal (mathematical) geometry produce extensions (porches) of different depths...

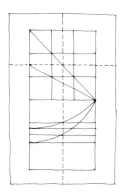

... so how can you choose which to use? The Golden Rectangle seems special and interesting, it has properties you might think of a magical and mysterious, so try using it for your house.

Extend the side walls, as best you can, to the ends of the Golden Rectangle. (The smaller squares also indicate where you might position columns to give additional support to your roof structure.)

Now you have a porch which, discounting the thicknesses of the walls, is, theoretically, a Golden Rectangle too, just like the house of which it is part. In your mind at least you can feel that you have produced a harmonic relationship between the proportions of the porch and those of the house as a whole.

You are asked to extend your walls 'as best you can' because you will find that your blocks do not exactly fit the extra length required by the Golden Rectangle. To follow its ideal geometry exactly you would have to modify the sizes of some of your blocks. You would have to swap the authority of the geometry of making for that of ideal geometry. You will doubtless already have been affected by the seductive fascination of ideal geometry as a means by which to make decisions about the dimensions and arrangements of elements in architecture, so you may well feel this modification of the geometry of making is a price worth paying.

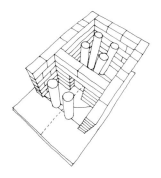

EXERCISE 9c. Cube.

We do not need to be content with playing games with ideal geometry in two dimensions. Architectural space is (at least) three dimensional. The 3 x 3 square may be elevated into three-dimensions by multiplying by three again: 3 x 3 x 3 = 27. Now you have a cube of space.

Build the walls of your house up until they are three units high.

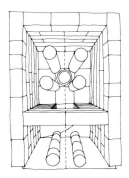

You will probably be amazed at how high the walls seem in relation to the square floor. But you have no choice but to follow the rule you have accepted – that of the cube. You have pledged obedience to ideal geometry in the belief that it will produce a space that can be intellectually (or perhaps ethically) identified as 'right' or aesthetically perceived as beautiful. You have ceded your judgement and will to a 'higher power' – that of mathematics.

EXERCISE 9d. Problems with wall thickness.

But in abdicating your own power of decision to that of mathematics (ideal geometry), you have not (as you might have wished) escaped problems associated with uncertainty. And these problems derive primarily from the intrusion of the thicknesses of materials into a geometry that would ideally like its boundaries to have no thickness at all.

For example, you may have decided the extent of your porch by applying the Golden Rectangle to the plan; but the plan of your porch is not a Golden Rectangle, not just because the blocks are not quite the right size but also because the thickness of the wall between it and the inner room intrudes into it. You might respond by suggesting that this party wall could be positioned straddling the line...

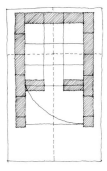

... but then neither the porch nor the inner room would have an ideal geometric

113

plan. You could extend the porch a little further (by the thickness of the wall) so that its plan did become a Golden Rectangle.

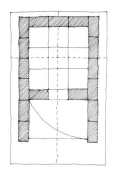

But then the plan of the whole (the inner room plus porch) would no longer be a Golden Rectangle and your aspirations to harmony would be lost.

These are problems in the two dimensional plan; they do not include the additional problems that occur when you draw the plan into three dimensions. When you contrive to enclose a space that is cubic, the form of the building enclosing that space

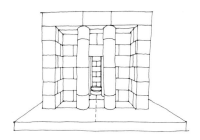

is not a cube; the ground (your board) accounts for one of the thicknesses of the bounding material. You could of course lift the building onto a podium of the same thickness as the walls.

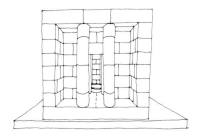

But then again, you might wish you had never started playing with ideal geometry at all! Maybe it is the road to hell rather than heaven. A preoccupation with ideal geometry and the aspiration to perfection draws attention away from considering the person and their possessions, activities, experiences...

Alternatively, you might see the quest for ideal geometry as a game worth playing; perhaps because it gives you a crutch, something to lean on, a system by which to make decisions; perhaps you feel it makes your plans look well-ordered; or, when presenting your work to others (your clients or critics), that it lends your work a credibility, an intellectual rigour (however spurious that might or might not be) that attracts or demands respect.

(See also pages 126-127.)

IN YOUR NOTEBOOK...

In your notebook... find and draw examples
of buildings that have been designed
according to the ideal geometry of
the square, cube, √2 rectangle, Golden
Rectangle.

Some examples are very easy to spot.
Shinichi Ogawa's Cubist House in Yamaguchi,
Japan (1990) is a glass cube.

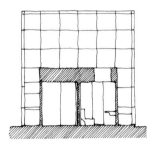

section

plan

Other examples you will have to analyse
more carefully. In doing this you will find
it useful to make yourself a transparent
diagram (on tracing paper or acetate) of
the principal rectangles used.

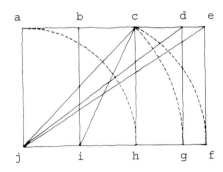

achj is a square;
adgj is a √2 rectangle;
aefj is a Golden Rectangle;
abij and bchi are double squares.

You could include a 3 x 2 rectangle too.

Mark in the diagonals of the various
rectangles. These will be useful. You
can overlay your transparent diagram on
plans you find in journals and books. The
diagonals will tell you if you have found
an example in which the architect has used
one of these rectangles in laying out their
work.

Your aim in doing this is to find which
architects have used ideal geometry in
their work and those who have not; and, in
the cases of those who have, to discover
how they played the game. You might also
wish to muse on the benefits that have
accrued to them by using ideal geometry
as a way of making decisions about the
positions, proportions and dimensions of
parts of their buildings and maybe those
buildings' relationships with their sites.

115

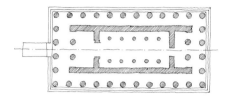

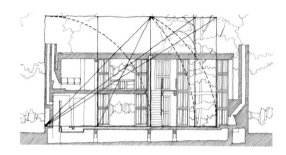

section

You will find that, for example, in designing the Farnsworth House, Mies van der Rohe did not use ideal geometry.

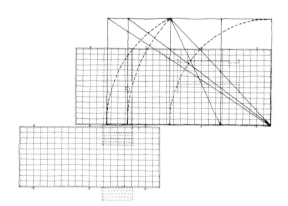

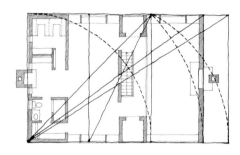

plan

It seems he was more interested in following the proportions of a particular ancient Greek temple (that of Aphaia at Aegina, top) and expressing it in a whole number of stone slabs on the floors of the platforms, i.e. through the geometry of making. The Farnsworth House is one of the case studies analysed in *Twenty Buildings Every Architect Should Understand*. You will find more there on Mies's attitude to geometry and the ways in which he lent his buildings a genetic integrity derived from factors other than ideal geometry.

Louis Kahn's Esherick House is another case study in *Twenty Buildings*. This is a building in which it appears the architect *has* used ideal geometry to determine the proportions of his plan.

You can see that the diagonal of the $\sqrt{2}$ rectangle in your diagram coincides with the diagonal of the plan of the house. It seems Kahn used ideal geometry in designing the section of the house too (top). A more detailed geometrical analysis is provided in *Twenty Buildings*.

It is not only in the twentieth century that ideal geometry has been used in designing architecture. As a device it is literally as old as the pyramids. Ideal geometry in architecture is not only a crutch that helps in making decisions about the sizes, proportions and positions of elements.

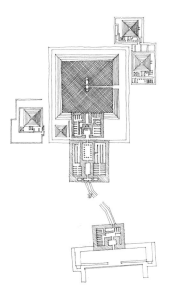

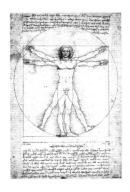

Egyptian pyramids were square in plan not only because they formalised the circle of place around the last resting place of the pharaoh within the solid matter of the rock from which it was built and oriented it to the four points of the compass, but also because the perfection of the square, elevated in the form of a pyramid, seemed in accord with the state of death.

Palladio's Villa Rotonda (sixteenth century) is square in plan too, though its doorway axes are oriented between the cardinal points of the compass.

The circle of place of the person is central to the composition of the Villa Rotonda but the ideal geometry of the building associates the human being at its centre with the idea of perfection. It also alludes to the belief, as illustrated in Leonardo da Vinci's famous drawing of Vitruvian Man (top), that the form of the perfect human being was ordered according to ideal geometry too.

The temples of ancient Greece appear to have been designed according to ideal geometry for aesthetic reasons, i.e. because it made them more harmonious visually, more beautiful. But the geometry of these building is so subtle it is often difficult to determine exactly how it was used. The elevation of this small temple seems, for example, to have been designed according to the square and perhaps the $\sqrt{2}$ rectangle, but not in an obvious or simplistic way.

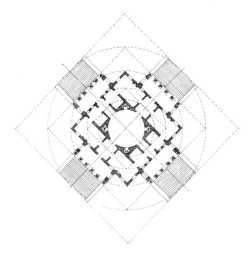

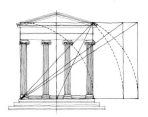

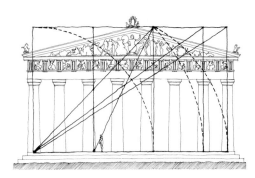

And the front of the Parthenon may be interpreted as having been designed according to the Golden Rectangle, but again not in an obvious or simplistic way.

You may read elsewhere (in A.W. Lawrence, *Greek Architecture*, pages 169-175 for example) of the subtle ways in which Greek architects gently curved or distorted some elements of the geometry of their temples to counter optical illusions such as: the apparent 'waisting' of columns with straight sides (countered by means of *entasis* - an almost imperceptible swelling of the column shaft); the apparent depression of a temple base (by making it gently convex); the apparent widening towards the top of a temple with perfectly vertical sides (by making those sides slope gently inwards); etc. These distortions or refinements are thought to have been done for aesthetic reasons - to make the temple appear more beautiful. They add a subtle nuance to (prompt intriguing questions about) the use of ideal geometry in architecture: if ideal geometry offers a formula for beauty in buildings then why should it need refinement? Maybe ideal

geometry is no more than a satisfying game for the architect, a system that helps in making decisions about proportions, relationships and dimensions, but which offers no clear benefit to the person.

Architects have used ideal geometry for thousands of years. In the sixteenth century it seems that Michelangelo used the geometry of the square and the Golden Rectangle as the basis for his design for the stair vestibule of the Laurentian Library in Florence.

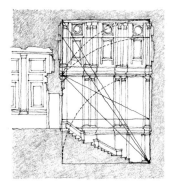

section

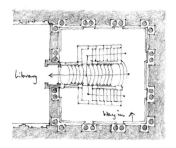

plan

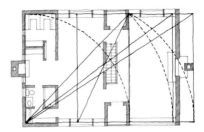

There are always uncertainties about identifying the ideal geometry according to which any particular design may (or may not) have been designed. In Exercise 9d we encountered some of the difficulties involved in accounting for wall thickness in a geometric scheme. The same difficulty afflicts the geometric analysis of plans and sections. It is not always easy to discern where exactly you should place your transparent diagram to reveal the hidden geometry of a plan or section.

For example, as well as there being a $\sqrt{2}$ rectangle apparent in the plan of Kahn's Esherick House, it seems, if you include the end chimneys, also to fit within a Golden Rectangle.

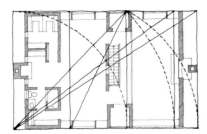

But the Golden Rectangle 'works' for the Esherick House in slightly different positions too.

A historian might become obsessed with identifying exactly which geometric composition Kahn actually used and scrutinise his drawings for clues. But within the context of learning how architecture works and exploring various ways in which it might be done it is enough to be reasonably sure that Kahn did use ideal geometry in laying out his work, and to consider carefully what it is that ideal geometry offers the architect (you) and those who use and experience buildings. You should explore using ideal geometry in your own work and decide whether or not it helps you achieve what you want or what is needed in particular circumstances. You will find that a surprisingly large number of architects through the centuries have used ideal geometry. Many of the twentieth century buildings examined in *Twenty Buildings Every Architect Should Understand* display its use when analysed. Mies van der Rohe was an exception. The danger, or perhaps it is a possibility with positive consequences, is that you too will become obsessed.

INTERLUDE: sphere

The sphere is a form you cannot make with your blocks. It is an ideal geometric form, a Platonic solid and, as such, an attractive proposition for realisation in architectural form.

The Pantheon (1) was built in Rome in the early second century CE.

The huge Newton Cenotaph (2) was designed by Étienne-Louis Boullée in the late eighteenth century but never built.

The Rose Center for Earth and Space (3) was built in the American Museum of Natural History in New York in 2000. It was designed by the Polshek Partnership and contains a spherical planetarium.

All three buildings, from different periods of history, manifest architecture based on the sphere. They all allude to the shape ascribed to the sky. They also illustrate problems architects encounter when trying to make spherical spaces. These problems involve conflicts between ideal geometry and some of the geometries of being. The first of these relates to the geometry of making; the second to the geometry of human movement; both relate to the consistently vertical force of gravity.

Hemispherical domes built in masonry or concrete gradually deviate the force of gravity down through the spherical fabric to the ground but the force acting on an upside-down dome is very different. Think of the shape of an under-inflated balloon resting on a table.

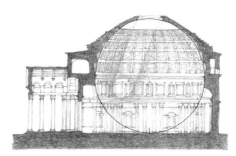

1

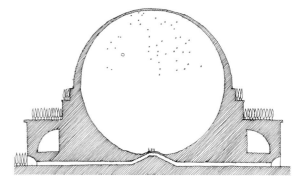

2

The top half will be approximately domelike while the bottom will be flattened against the table's surface.

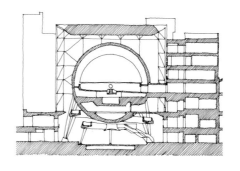

3

The Pantheon deals with this problem by replacing the bottom half of the sphere with a cylinder – the vertical walls take the weight of the dome down to the ground. Newton's Cenotaph relies on a huge mass of masonry wrapped around the lower half of the sphere to give it stability. Being built of a spherical steel framework the planetarium in the Rose Center for Earth and Space has more the integrated structure of an egg. Its lower half is supported by props that hold the sphere in space.

The sphere may be a super representation of the circle of place, expanding it into the third dimension. But whereas it is possible for each of us to occupy the centre of a circle drawn on the ground and its expansion into space as a cylinder, it is impossible without a trapeze to occupy the centre of a large spherical space. Also, it is easy for us to move around, as actors in the circular orkestra of an ancient Greek theatre, on the horizontal ground defined by a circle of place. But a built sphere of space has only a small area in which, under the influence of the force of gravity, we would feel able to move around. Think of trying to walk around in the base of a wok (Chinese cooking pan); a surface good for skateboarding is not going to be good for moving around on foot. In a perfect sphere there is only one infinitely small spot of its surface that is horizontal.

Again, the Pantheon deals with this problem by replacing the bottom half of the sphere with a cylinder which has a circular but horizontal floor on which we may easily walk. That infinitely small area of the sphere that would be horizontal is marked as the centre of the circular floor, directly under the oculus that admits a shaft of sunlight to track around the space.

The interior of the Newton Cenotaph was not intended as a space in which to move around; it would have been powerful enough just to experience the space from the centre, near the point at which the memorial to Isaac Newton (the 'inventor' of gravity) would have been.

The planetarium in the Rose Center deals with this problem in a different way. A horizontal floor is built approximately across the middle of the spherical space. In this way, while the exterior is seen as a sphere, the interior is experienced as a hemisphere.

Spheres present challenges regarding entrance too. The Pantheon has less problem with a doorway than the other two examples illustrated here. The doorway gives access into the cylinder at ground level. But even so there is a slight conflict between the axial rectangular geometry of the portico (porch) and the radial geometry of the circular plan.

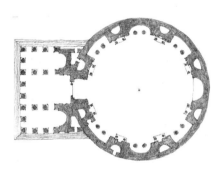

Boullée solved the problem by entering the Newton Cenotaph from underneath and the lowest point of the sphere of space. The Rose Centre planetarium is entered across a bridge near its midriff.

Like many examples in which ideal geometry is imposed on architectural form, conflicts arise with geometries of being: the way people are made and move; the ways in which gravity works; and the ways in which materials can be constructed into buildings.

EXERCISE 10: symmetry and asymmetry

While you were collecting (for the preceding 'Notebook' exercise) examples governed by ideal geometry, you may have noticed different strategies dividing plans into constituent rooms or spaces. We have already explored the geometry of planning in Exercise 8 but here are more issues to consider, to do with spatial hierarchy, movement and relationships with the world outside.

The tendency through history has been to associate ideal geometry with axial symmetry. Axial symmetry can easily be confused with the doorway axis because they are often allied. But axial symmetry, whether in an elevation or a plan, is different in that it constitutes an intellectual idea expressed primarily in the abstract drawings that architects do - plans and elevations - and as such is distinct from a phenomenological effect; i.e. it is only when you look at an architect's plan that you can see whether or not it is arranged symmetrically about an axis; but you experience the power of a doorway axis when you stand before it.

The symmetrical axis is a factor in ideal geometry. It has been a bone of contention through the twentieth century. Symmetry and asymmetry suggest different attitudes to hierarchy and movement through the rooms of a building. They can also lead onto different relationships between the inside and the outside world.

EXERCISE 10a. Axis of symmetry.

A doorway axis can become an instrument of spatial organisation. We have seen this in previous exercises when, for example, we laid out a house with a bed on each side of the axis and a hearth at its focus.

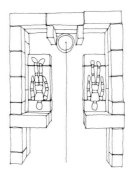

We have seen too that this can lead conceptually to the classic form of the temple, mosque or church, with its sense of direction, movement along the axis to a point of culmination.

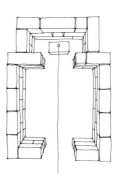

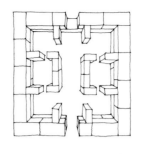
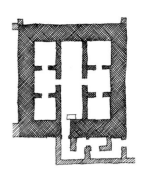

When we draw an axis, whether or not it emanates from a doorway, it can become not just a line of movement and focus but also a principle for spatial organisation. Static human beings, standing to attention, are symmetrical; so perhaps the plans and elevations of buildings should be too?

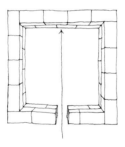

There are many ways in which the rooms of, for example, a square plan might be laid out symmetrically about an axis. Most classical and 'Beaux Arts' follow this rule. (You can look up 'Beaux Arts Architecture' on Wikipedia.)

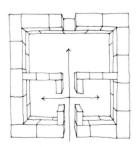
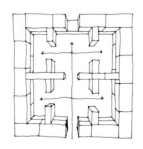

All define a central axis along which one moves towards the most important room and off which one accesses secondary rooms.

Try as many variations as you can with your blocks. You might, for example, layout a plan based on your 3 x 3 square grid, like that of the core of the Necromanteion (above) built perhaps three thousand years ago in ancient Greece. Or you might organise your plan around a main central room as in Palladio's Villa Rotonda (on page 117) or other buildings influenced by it such as Chiswick Villa (below, designed by Lord Burlington and William Kent in the late 1720s).

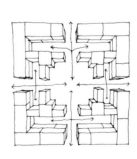
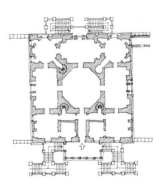

Symmetry, as an architectural idea, is a rule that what happens on one side of an axis should be mirrored on the other. It is a powerful rule, often associated with hierarchy and authority, but like all rules it invites subversion.

123

AN OBSERVATION: the (im)possibility of perfection?

An aspiration associated with the use of ideal geometry and its acceptance as holding authority over design is the desire to achieve perfect form. Similarly an aspiration associated with the use of axial symmetry is a desire to achieve perfect balance or correspondence of parts. But are either ideal geometry or perfect symmetry possible in this world? Are they, as Plato suggested, ideals ('forms') to which human beings might aspire but never quite reach. Are ideal geometry and perfect symmetry possible? Some instances suggest that they are not.

Problems of imperfection.

At the beginning of Exercise 9a we drew a 3 x 3 square.

Using a piece of graph paper as an underlay we might have drawn the squares freehand, so it would be understandable if the lines were not quite straight and the squares not quite square. The 3 x 3 square is born of a perfect idea but in realisation is far from perfect. This example shows the difference between

an ideal ('form' - square) and its realisation. If we had used a ruler the lines would have been straighter but even so the measuring would have been slightly inaccurate and the lines would have varied in thickness, however careful we tried to be. Even if we had used a computer graphics program and taken great care to make the square exactly the same number of pixels in each direction its representation on the screen would be distorted.

However much care one might take, our attempt to realise a perfect square in reality is always going to have some imperfections, even if only at an atomic level. Certainly you will find it impossible to make a perfect square with your building blocks.

Even though they were probably quite accurately cut, there are likely to be slight inconsistencies in their sizes, which, when the blocks are put together, are compounded. The same limitations apply in three dimensions, when you try to build a perfect cube out of your blocks.

The problem of imperfection afflicts attempts to achieve perfect axial symmetry too. It is very difficult, impossible, to arrange your model person in a perfectly symmetrical stance.

It is likely that in its manufacture the opposing arms, legs, joints... are not quite exactly mirrored or do not operate in exactly the same way.

Probably the nearest real people come to adopting a perfectly symmetrical stance is when they stand to attention. But even then it is likely that their own bodies are not quite symmetrical. One eye or ear will be slightly higher, one foot slightly bigger, than the other. Nobody's perfect.

We spend the vast majority of our time in asymmetrical poses.

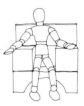

So when we stand a person on our cube (turning it into a place – a place to stand and orate)...

... we find our attempts to achieve perfection in ideal geometry and axial symmetry thwarted in a variety of ways: the imperfections of the blocks and person; the asymmetry of the way the blocks are laid and the pose of the person. Maybe value lies in our aspiration to perfection rather than in its (unattainable) achievement? Maybe beauty attaches to an interplay between symmetry and asymmetry (as in beat and melody in music), rather than one or the other?

Problems of thickness (again).

Start with the 3 x 3 square. Increase the thickness of the lines of the square (as if they were walls drawn in plan).

Yes, the lines are not quite straight and the square probably not quite perfectly square. But we have another problem too. Where exactly is the square?

Does the extent of the square stretch to the outer edges of the lines, is it contained by the inner edges of the lines, or is it defined by the centre lines of the lines (dashed in the drawing)? (This problem afflicts ball games: in soccer the thickness of the line is inside the field of play while in rugby it is outside; in tennis a ball may merely touch the very outside of the line and still be counted 'in'.) This problem afflicts the definition of an ideal geometric figure (square, circle, Golden Rectangle...) however thin the lines may be.

Now divide the square into its nine component squares, using lines of the same thickness. Let's say the drawing is very magnified and lines are one pixel thick, so that in a computer drawing we could not possibly get the lines to be any thinner. This is like the plan of a nine roomed building with no doorways, and a pixel is equivalent to the thickness of a brick wall.

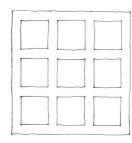 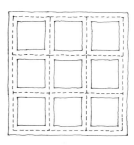

Now the problem of the definition of the square is compounded. We can mark in the centre lines of the lines. It appears we have nine equal squares making one big square, but is that really the case?

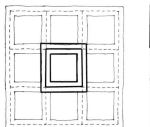 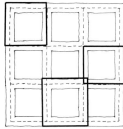 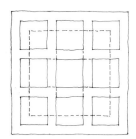

We have one central square which remains square whether you define it by the inner, outer or centre lines of its bounding lines. But, whether at the corners or in the middle of each side, definition of the squares becomes more problematic.

Now measure along the outer edges of the big square, dividing them as exactly as you can into three. Join these third points across the square.

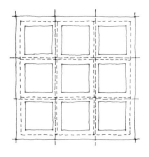

They do not match the centre lines of the lines defining the smaller squares. We begin to see that we do not have a big square composed simply of nine equal smaller squares. We have something more complex instead.

This problem arises when trying to compose buildings according to ideal geometry. It can also be a reason why it is often difficult to identify, by analysis, which ideal geometric figures an architect has used in composing a building and how they have determined dimensions and relationships.

The only way to approach the sought for perfection is to eliminate the thickness of the lines and push the smaller squares right up tight to each other.

To do this properly we cannot leave any trace of lines because however thin those lines might be the problem of thickness remains. So the square disappears.

The only place a perfect square may exist is in our minds, as an idea. It cannot exist as a drawing printed in a book or even as a very precise drawing on a computer screen. It cannot exist as a building with walls of real material.

INTERLUDE: 9 Square Grid House

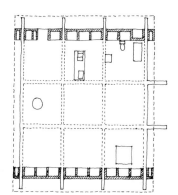

1 plan

The Japanese architect, Shigeru Ban, has
designed a house based on a 3 x 3 square in
which the thickness of walls can be made to
disappear. It is the 9 Square Grid House, built
in Japan in 1997 (1 and 2). The house has
partitions that may be moved (on rails) out of
the way into slots in the walls. The two glazed
end walls may also be pushed aside opening the
house to the outside. The partitions may be
positioned to divide the space in various ways.
With the space completely open, the bathroom
and kitchen fittings and the bed stand open to
the whole house and the world. Partitions may
be positioned to provide privacy as required.
Various spatial arrangements are possible
(within the limitations of the grid) according
to circumstances.

Even so, the geometry of the space does not
avoid the problem of thickness (see previous
'Observation'). Space has to be allocated
between the subsidiary squares for the rails
on which the partitions run. Rails are not
needed along the side walls (which house storage
cupboards) so the basic space of the 9 Square
Grid House is not perfectly square. Also,
because of their own thickness, when extended
the partitions do not create a perfectly
straight wall but one that is stepped.

Perhaps Shigeru Ban was not so interested in
geometric perfection. The idea of the 9 Square
Grid House seems to allude to the traditional
Japanese house (3) with its sliding screens that
may be pushed aside to make open spaces and
to open rooms to the outside. The geometry of
spaces in the traditional Japanese house avoids
the problem of thickness by concentrating on
making the spaces between walls a whole number
of mats, each of which is a double square. These
mats are called 'tatami'. An eight tatami room
is therefore square whereas a six tatami room
will be a 4 x 3 rectangle.

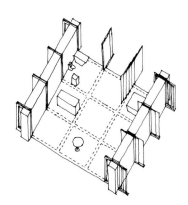

2

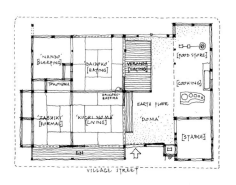

3

Forces beyond your control.

Designing form according to ideal geometry may express a desire to achieve perfection, intellectual or aesthetic. It might derive from a human aspiration to surpass nature as a creative force. Nature's products always seem in some way to be flawed or deviate from the perfect model. Maybe human beings should see themselves as the agents of perfection, bringing order and discipline to the apparently mindless and indifferent natural creation. Some see this humanist attitude as heroism; others as hubris – misdirected, cocky and ultimately futile arrogance.

We do not have to interpret ideal geometry in this philosophical way. It can have a more prosaic role in doing architecture. When you are faced with the blank sheet of paper or computer screen and are setting out to fill it with a design, beginning by drawing a square (for example) provides a starting point and a 'hand rail' to guide you through the design process. It leads you into a system for design, based in geometry, according to which you can make design decisions.

Ideal geometry may help you make design decisions you can think of as 'right' but, nevertheless, it is hermetic, sealed off in its own realm (of uncertain location, see pages 153–154 of *Analysing Architecture*). In its perfect form, ideal geometry can

only exist as an idea. But even when we approach perfect form in building it is likely to be disrupted when it encounters the real world.

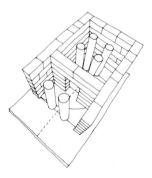

Here is an example. When I had built the model for Exercise 9b (above) my wife walked past carrying a towel.

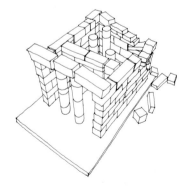

The corner of the towel brushed the model causing part of it to collapse. The form of my building changed; it had been affected by a force beyond my control. It

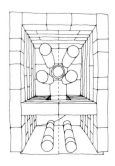 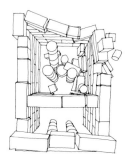

acquired a form that I could never achieve by conscious decision. Even if I knocked the model deliberately I would knock it in a predetermined place, harder or softer than the towel... and the result would be different. I would know that I had done the damage deliberately. Even if, after I had wiped it away, I rebuilt the model in its damaged state, carefully and precisely, the result would be conceptually different from the model damaged by being brushed accidentally by the towel.

Think of other forces that afflict buildings and change their form undermining any perfection they might have or aspire to. These include: the weather – rain, wind, ice, sun...; seismological forces – earthquakes, tsunami, volcanic activity...; the growth of plants; and the actions of other people – damage through use or alteration, vandalism, war...

As an architect your attitude to the effects of these forces beyond your control evokes Hamlet's quandary: 'Whether 'tis nobler in the mind to suffer the slings and arrows of outrageous fortune, or to take arms against a sea of troubles, and by opposing end them?' But a third way is to exploit the effects of forces beyond your control for aesthetic or poetic effect.

Some of the most subtle and powerful works of architecture play on this blend of accident and control, nature and order imposed by the mind. This is easily seen in gardens where designs imposed by a mind are realised in the form of plants that grow according to their own natures. Some Picturesque gardens of the eighteenth and nineteenth centuries, such as Scotney Old Castle in Kent, benefited from having a ruined building as the focus of their composition. In Italy, Ninfa is a large (20 acre) garden created within the ruins of an old city deserted in the fourteenth century.

This attitude can inform the treatment of old buildings too. At the Castelvecchio in Verona (in the 1950s) the architect Carlo Scarpa allowed remnants of different periods of the building's history to contribute to his design. And in the Neues Museum in Berlin, which was reopened in 2009 after lying in ruins since the Second World War, the architect David Chipperfield retained marks of war damage as a reminder of the building's past. You can see these gardens and buildings at:

Scotney – www.nationaltrust.org.uk/main/w-vh/w-visits/w-findaplace/w-scotneycastlegarden/w-scotneycastlegarden-history.htm

Ninfa – www.fondazionecaetani.org/visita_ninfa.php

Castelvecchio – www.comune.verona.it/castelvecchio/cvsito/

Neues Museum – www.neues-museum.de/

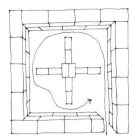

EXERCISE 10b. Subverting axial symmetry.

Try disrupting the power of the axis as the organising principle of symmetry by occupying the centre or blocking the doorway axis.

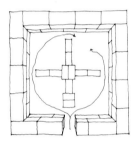

The plan may still be symmetrical but its symmetry is subverted by the effect on the person whose movement is diverted to one side or other by the obstruction. In this way the plan is no longer experienced as symmetrical but as a circular route.

Freedom from the authority of the axis of symmetry might be achieved merely by moving the doorway.

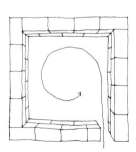

An asymmetrical entrance makes axial movement impossible and can reinforce a circular or wandering route.

In his tower house at Riva San Vitale (1973), for example, Mario Botta established a generally spiral route through the building by starting it with an off centre entrance bridge on the top floor. The house was organised according to an eccentric ideal geometry based on the square and Golden Rectangle.

You can (roughly) model the idea of Botta's spiral route using your blocks. The route leads to a spiral stair that runs down near the centre of the tower.

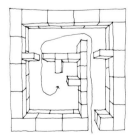

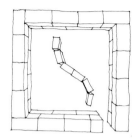
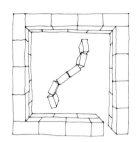

Starting with a simple square of space defined by a bounding wall, experiment with different ways of dividing space which are free of the dominating power of the axis. Begin with a doorway at a corner rather than centrally positioned.

You can divide the space with a diagonal wall.

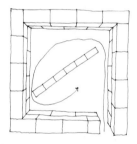

This (with a few additional subtleties) is effectively what Sverre Fehn did when (in 1998) he was faced with the challenge of arranging the interior space of Palladio's Basilica in Vicenza for an exhibition of his own work.

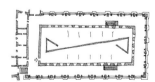

Your diagonal wall might even be curved rather than straight. Notice how one's experience of the spaces would be different related to the precise position of the

wall. In the left drawing above you enter a narrow space past a probably unnoticed doorway to your left, gradually reaching a wider space; whereas in the right drawing above you enter directly into a large space, eventually finding a doorway, one way or the other, into the more secluded second space.

You could organise your space with a free composition of orthogonal walls, as Mies van der Rohe might have done.

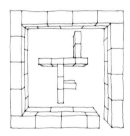

This might lead you to wonder why your walls need to be attached to each other and why they need to be confined within the bounding wall. Maybe the internal walls might begin to 'escape' through the doorway.

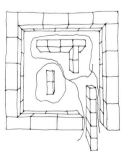

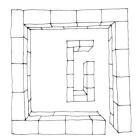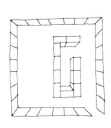

Perhaps your free composition of walls 'decide' they no longer need the bounding walls. They can define, or suggest, circles of place on their own...

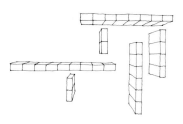

... perhaps with the help of transparent glass walls that do not obscure views to the outside world.

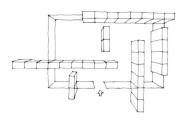

You can imagine how these spaces might be used, perhaps as: an entrance lobby; a dining space; a kitchen; a living room; a small study.

You might divide your space with a core, perhaps containing a bathroom, a closet, a kitchen... (top right). With glass rather than masonry bounding walls, this was the idea of Mies's Farnsworth House (see

Twenty Buildings Every Architect Should Understand) and of related projects such as the Fifty by Fifty Foot House...

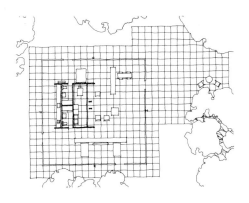

... in which a core contains plant room and bathrooms but also plays its part in dividing up the space of the house between kitchen, bedroom and living spaces.

In his courtyard houses, Mies also experimented with what might be thought of as close to the inverse architectural idea - i.e. dividing the space within a solid perimeter with glass walls.

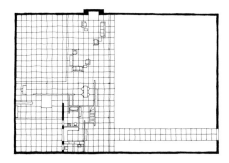

In his extension to the National Architecture Museum in Oslo (2008)...

... Sverre Fehn made a glass enclosure with roof supported on four columns, surrounded by a separate bounding screen wall. This he broke open in places to provide specific views out. You can try the same with your blocks.

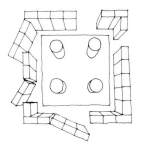

The corner entrance avoids the possible axial relationship with the four columns. Notice how the nature of the space, its implied dynamic (i.e. how you tend to move into and through it), changes when you move the doorway to the centre of one side.

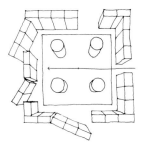

Even though the breaks in the outer screen walls may remain asymmetrical, the central doorway provokes an axis related to the centre of the space. In doing so it changes the nature of the space. The doorway in the corner is less deterministic; it suggests wandering into a space in which exhibits, their cases and stands, may be laid out in many informal ways.

There are multifarious ramifications to asymmetry in planning. You can explore them endlessly, finding those that appear to relate to programme, site or provide an engaging experience.

IN YOUR NOTEBOOK...

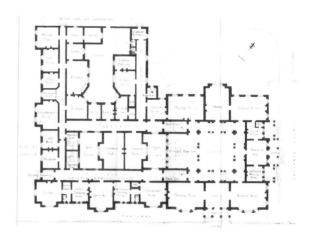

This is a hypothetical plan for an 'English Gentleman's House' taken from Robert Kerr's book of that title published in the nineteenth century. Why is part of it symmetrical and part asymmetrical?

In your notebook... collect and draw examples of plans that are symmetrical and others that are not.

You will find both symmetry and asymmetry in all periods of architecture. You only need to collect a few examples of each. You should collect plans of some buildings that you can also visit. Think very carefully about the differences. In each particular case consider issues such as:

• is symmetry merely a graphic game being played by the architect to make what might appear a balanced drawing?

• what are the implications for movement and the experience of the person; how are these different in the case of symmetrical and asymmetrical plans? (Think about direction and wandering.)

• what happens when you compose a number of small symmetries within an asymmetrical whole?

• do you feel different in a symmetrical space as compared with an asymmetrical space; in what way do you feel different?

• how might symmetry or asymmetry in the layout of spaces affect your ability to know where you are, to find your way about a building...?

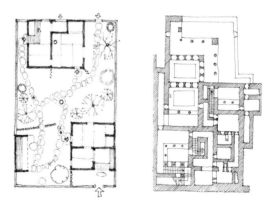

On the left is a plan of a traditional Japanese tea house. On the right is the plan of the part of the ancient Minoan palace at Knossos thought to be the Royal Apartments. Both avoid emphasising doorway axes. What might this asymmetry indicate about attitudes to hierarchy in each case?

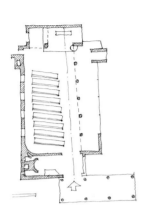

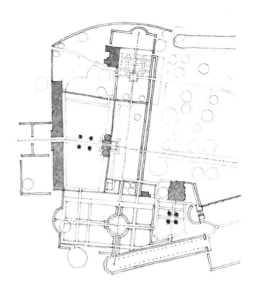

How would your experience of Erik Bryggman's Cemetery Chapel at Turku (1941) be different from that of Erik Gunnar Asplund's Woodland Chapel (1918)?

Above is the layout of Sissinghurst garden, formed amongst older buildings in the early twentieth century by Vita Sackville-West and Harold Nicholson. Below is the plan of Frank Lloyd Wright's Martin Residence (1904). Both use axes and symmetry within a larger asymmetrical whole. How do you think their architects' attitudes to a person's experience differed?

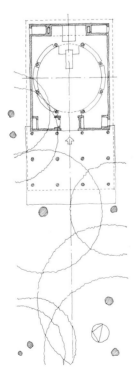

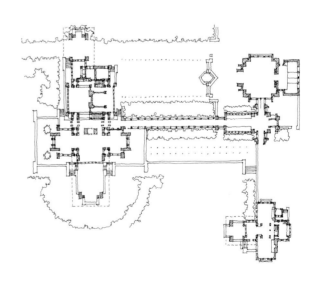

EXERCISE 11: playing with geometry

You, like other architects, can play other games with ideal geometry. These include: layering geometries one on another; breaking geometries; and distorting geometries. With these we are rapidly approaching the limits of what can be explored through the medium of your children's building blocks and bread board.

EXERCISE 11a. Layering geometry.

It might not be something that would occur to you when building directly in the real world, but when you begin to draw plans for buildings before erecting them it is easy to allow graphic devices to enter in.

One can for example imagine (mischievously and entirely without evidence) Andrea Palladio idly twiddling a pair of compasses as he tried to come up with an idea for his newly won commission to build a grand house for the retired priest Paolo Almerico.

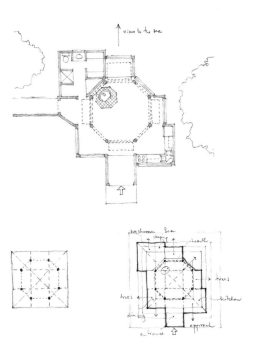

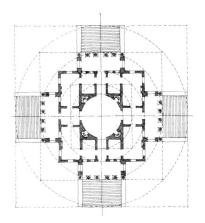

In his design for the Johnson House at Sea Ranch (on the North California coast, 1965) William Turnbull began with a square, which he related to the geometry of making (in timber). He then added to and took away from this square in response to the setting and to the activities the house was to accommodate.

By concentric circles and squares, Palladio grew the armature for Villa Rotonda around a single centre. But he could have layered his geometry in many different ways, breaking free of the centre and its related axes of symmetry.

137

You might for example dislocate squares so they create a composition of eccentric and different sized spaces.

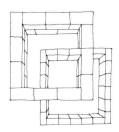

You could then remove portions of the walls to make the spaces you need. You might replace a corner with a column (to support the roof or wall above) and make some walls of glass to give light and views. (You can add your own windows.)

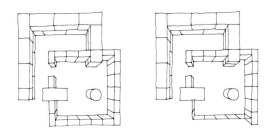

You can imagine this rather simplistic example serving to accommodate an entrance lobby, kitchen and living room, or perhaps a bathroom and bedroom. The result is similar to the plan of the Umemiya House built in the early 1980s by the Japanese architect Tadao Ando.

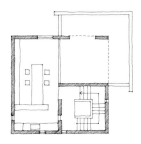

upper plan

lower plan

It has a bedroom, shower room and living space on the lower floor, and a dining room, kitchen and partly shaded outdoor terrace on the upper floor. The stair between the two occupies a corner of the larger square. One square is displaced from the other at an angle of 45° so that almost all the spaces of the house are also square, except the shower room, which has to make way for the entrance passage, and the dining room which is a double square.

You can layer other ideal geometric figures too; a square with a circle for example.

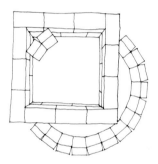

Here too you might remove portions to allow access between the spaces you wish to create.

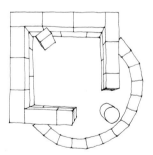

This might be a room with a corner hearth and a circular balcony protruding from the opposite corner.

Ando's Museum of Literature in Himeji, Japan, (1989-91) is based on a composition of a circle and square (below), though one that becomes more complex than the preceding model.

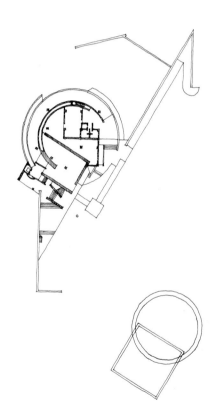

You can experiment with layering other figures for yourself, using your blocks or in drawing.

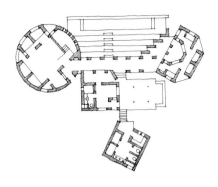

In his design for the Childrens' Retreat in Damdana, India (1999, left), Gautam Bhatia has used various geometric figures. The building is built in stone and brick and generally also follows the geometry of making.

EXERCISE 11b. Twisting geometry.

You might add a twist (literally) by turning one square at an angle to the other.

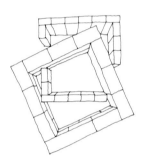

Again you would have to remove portions of walls to provide access from one space to another, and perhaps make some walls of glass.

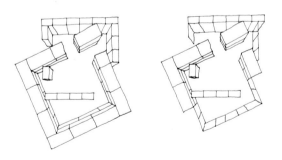

This could be a living room with sun lounge, triangular cupboard, and small study... accessed through a triangular entrance lobby.

Though with additional subtleties, this is the approach used by Ando in his design for the Minolta Seminar Building in Kobe, Japan (also 1989-91).

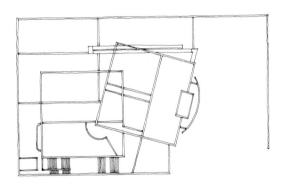

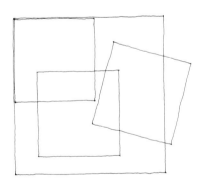

The plan of the Minolta Seminar Building is based on a collection of squares, one of which is twisted to break the predictability of the geometry.

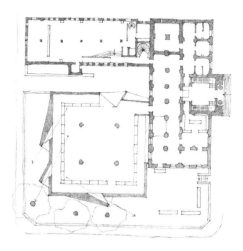

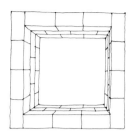

EXERCISE 11c. Breaking ideal geometry.

Alternatively, you could look at what happens when you fracture geometry, maybe by dislocating a portion (1), by biting a piece off (2) or by breaking it into pieces (3).

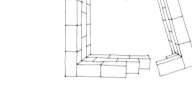

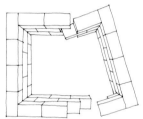

1

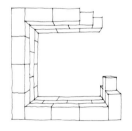

2

3

In his extension to the National Architecture Museum in Olso (see also page 134) Sverre Fehn fractured the outer screen wall around the glass box of the gallery, to allow the controlled views out.

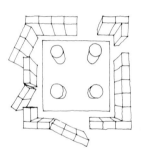

The architect Alvaro Siza built the Casa Carlos Beires in the mid 1970s. You can see its conception in its plan. It is as if a corner of a 4 x 3 rectangle has been broken off, with a zig zag glass wall like a tear across the breach in the wall.

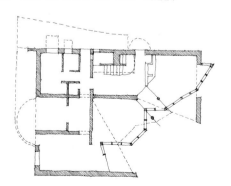

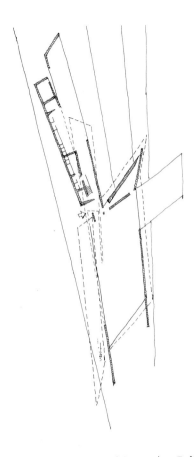

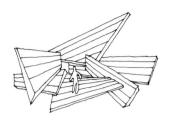

It begins to evoke the idea of architecture returning to the formless pile of blocks from which we began these exercises.

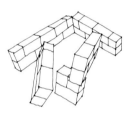

The 'breaking' manifest in Zaha Hadid's Vitra Fire Station is more drastic.

It is as if the elements of an orthogonal building have been broken apart and recomposed according to a warped alternative geometry that diverges from the orthogonal. (See *Analysing Architecture*, pages 167–169.)

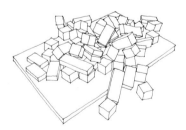

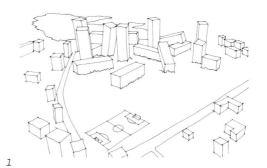

1

We tend to think of broken geometries
as associated with damage and destruction.
The orthogonal geometry of buildings
is disrupted by disaster – earthquake,
tsunami, hurricane, war...

Dutch architects MVRDV have explored
disruption of geometries aligned with the
vertical and horizontal in competition
entries such as their proposal for the
Tirana Rocks project in Albania (*1*, 2009)
and for Motor City in Spain (*2*, 2007). Both
are compositions of blocks arranged as if
tumbled onto the ground. Their disrupted
geometry is reminiscent of the leaning
house in the Bomarzo Gardens in Italy (*3*,
sixteenth century). All challenge our
expectations that the walls of buildings be
vertical and their floors horizontal. They
adhere to the geometry of making, but at
an angle. The floors of the leaning house
in Bomarzo slope, making the experience
of being inside strange. Both MVRDV
competition proposals include habitable
spaces so their floors would have to be
horizontal. The leaning geometry of all
three examples contrasts with the general
horizontality of the surfaces on which
we walk (and, in the top example, the
surface of the lake behind), the general
verticality of people and trees and the
orthogonality of nearby buildings (and, in
one case, the adjacent football pitch).

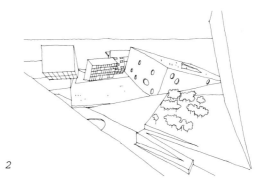

2

3

143

EXERCISE 11d. More complex geometries.

Mathematics, or the way in which the consistent force of gravity (which, according to Newtonian physics, acts according to formulae that can be expressed in mathematics) exerts its power, can produce geometric forms more complex than the circle, square or rectangle. Natural growth too sometimes appears to follow mathematical formulae. Here are two examples for you to experiment with: the catenary curve; and the spiral.

Catenary curve

The catenary curve is, put simply (without the mathematical formula), the curve of a piece of string or chain hanging from its two ends (1). Because it is a curve generated by the force of gravity the catenary also, when inverted, makes a strong form for an arch. It is the form of the Gateway Arch in St Louis (2).

You can try building a catenary arch with your blocks. You will need to make 'centering' to support your arch temporarily while you are building it. You can do this by tracing a catenary curve (downloaded from the internet) onto card. Cut this out and form your arch around it. You can use 'tacky' putty to fill the joints and stick the blocks together.

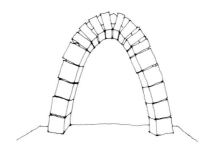

1

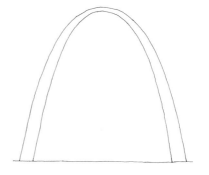

2

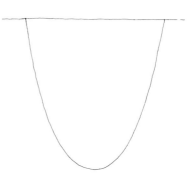

3

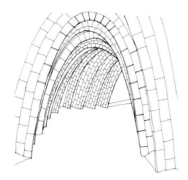

The Spanish architect Antonio Gaudi used catenary arches in his buildings. This drawing (above) shows the arches built in brick in the attic space of his Casa Milà in Barcelona (1910). Gaudi experimented with complex catenary models - hanging weights from loops of string - when deciding on the shapes of the vaults for his much grander project for the Sagrada Familia.

Spiral

The spiral is the form of some types of shell. It is a form of growth.

It has been used by architects too. You can describe a spiral on your board using a pencil and a piece of string. Take a cylindrical block and stand it at the centre of the board. Fixing one end of the string to the block, wrap it around the cylinder. Tie the other end to the pencil. As you unwind the string you can trace a spiral on the board.

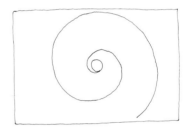

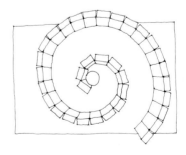

Then build your spiral with blocks.

145

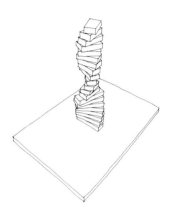

Zvi Hecker's apartment building the
Ramat Gan suburb of Tel Aviv in Israel is
a complex and broken spiral of squares and
circles (below).

You can build a three dimensional spiral
- a helix - too. Twist each block by the
same amount as you build a tower. This is
effectively the form of a spiral staircase,
as found in the towers of medieval castles.

Spirals have been used by more recent
architects too.

The best known 'spiral' building of the
twentieth century is no doubt Frank Lloyd
Wright's Guggenheim Art Museum in New York
(1959).

section

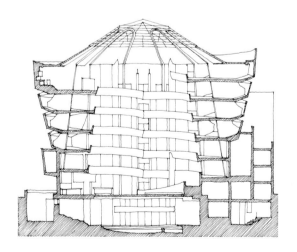

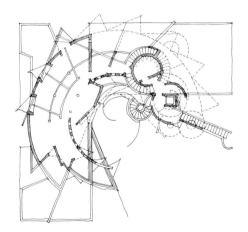

plan

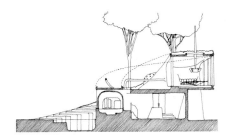

section (at a different scale)

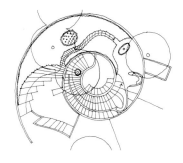

top level

Ushida Findlay's House for the Third Millennium (1994, which has not been built) is formed by a spiral that winds up to a roof terrace and then back down to the ground floor.

And Daniel Libeskind's unbuilt proposal for an extension to the Victoria and Albert Museum in London, called 'The Spiral', was reputedly inspired by a folded strip of stiff paper.

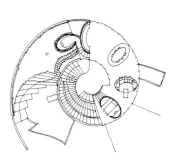

middle level

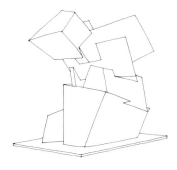

As in the case of the sphere and the leaning blocks of MVRDV, the floor becomes problematic in Libeskind's Spiral.

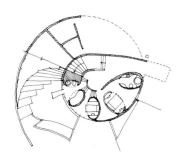

ground level

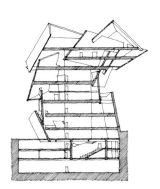

In Wright's Guggenheim the floor ramps gently upwards through the full height of the building. In Ushida Findlay's House for the Millenium it is formed of a stair that counterpoints the horizontal living floors (which have curved skirtings). In Libeskind's section the floors cut across the irregular internal space of the building leaving the distorted spiral form more apparent from the outside.

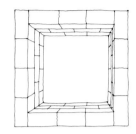

Möbius strip

Architects have used many different
geometric figures (in a addition to the
square, circle etc., and the catenary
curve and spiral) as the basis on which to
generate the design of buildings: pyramids;
prisms; ellipses; parabolas; hyperbolas...
Not only Libeskind has been inspired by
folded paper. Ben van Berkel of UN Studio
conceived a house based on the Möbius
strip, which has only one surface (above).
You can make one by cutting a strip of
paper and twisting one end a half turn then
sticking the ends together. The Möbius
House in Amsterdam (1998, below) has loops
of space that relate to the life of the
family living in it.

EXERCISE 11e. Distorting geometry.

The strange, unorthodox, weird... attracts
attention. Distortion adds strangeness. It
includes effects such as: making buildings
appear as if seen through a distorting lens
or in a distorting mirror; making surfaces
appear warped, wrinkled or melted; making
buildings with fluid, liquid forms. These
effects have been made easier to achieve by
computer software.

There is a limit to the extent to which
you can experiment with these effects using
your blocks. The blocks' own geometry of
making is incompatible with the free curves
needed. In the following drawings I have
smoothed out the lines of the models into
curves. I have also used tacky putty to
vary the thicknesses of the joints between
blocks or to make elements lean from the
vertical. Even with the limitations of
the materials to hand, it is possible
to experience some of the possibilities
of making architecture free from the
restraints imposed by the geometry of
making.

For example, constructing a block model
free from the authority of the rectangle
makes the process more sculptural. No
longer is the position and orientation of
each block predicted by the rectangular
geometry it shares with all its fellow
blocks. Each is positioned in its own

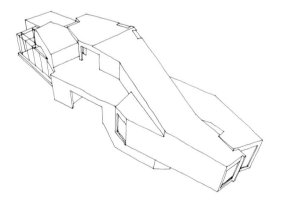

individual way according to your eye and judgement. There is no rule other than your aesthetic sensibility. You curve and slope your walls and roofs free of constraints.

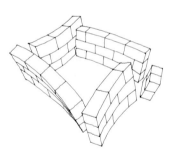

The freedom (which is infinitely greater when using computer software than wooden blocks) seems compelling; it is certainly seductive. Shapes become possible that would otherwise be inconceivable. But, as in the case of other non-orthogonal geometries, results can find themselves in conflict, not only with the geometry of making (which may be overcome by the power of computer software) but also with geometries that cannot be modified

– those of gravity, the person, furniture and doorways; aspects of architecture related to the geometries of being. Apart from the complexity of construction there is no problem giving a roof or ceiling an irregular curving geometry. It can however be problematic positioning beds and cupboards in irregularly shaped rooms and against curving walls.

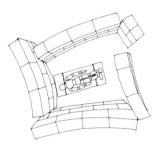

And, even though we human beings might enjoy strolling over hills and down dales, we find it uncomfortable living in spaces with uneven floors that disturb our balance.

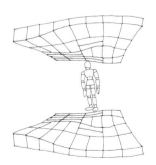

IN YOUR NOTEBOOK...

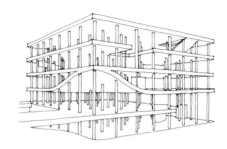

In your notebook... collect examples of buildings with distorted geometries.

Effects of distortion have been used for amusement, in fairground attractions such as 'The House that Jack Built', or to attract attention for commercial reasons such as in the Krzywy Domek (Crooked House) built in Sopot, Poland (below, 2004) by Szotynscy & Zaleski, which is primarily a distorted façade.

The Polish Crooked House has horizontal floors but, in their design for the Dutch Pavilion in the Hanover Expo (right, 2000), each floor of which simulated a different type of landscape, architects MVRDV made one floor with a rolling hilly ground surface.

MVRDV also experimented with a distorted floor plane in their design for the headquarters of the VPRO broadcasting organisation in Hilversum, in the Netherlands (1997, above).

You may also recall (from descriptions in *Doorway* and *Twenty Buildings Every Architect Should Understand*) that in the Church of St Peter, Klippan, Sigurd Lewerentz made the floor uneven, perhaps in recollection of the floor of San Marco in Venice but perhaps also to provoke the slight unsteadiness of being on the deck of a ship.

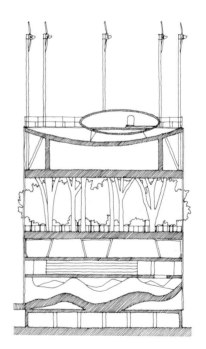

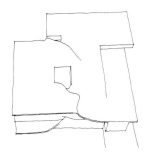

The best known example of distortion is Frank Gehry's Guggenheim Museum in Bilbao, Spain (1997, above). The sculpturally distorted form of its polished titanium cladding is credited with having transformed the economy of the city by attracting multitudes to see its sensational contrast with the orthodox (and generally orthogonal) city surroundings.

Many architects have explored the potential of the complex curved, distorted, geometries made possible with computer software.

And the Torus House, Columbia County, New York by Preston Scott Cohen in 1999.

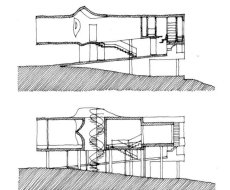

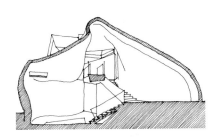

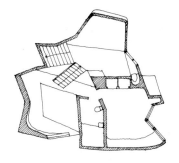

The former has a free, almost amoebic, form (but with horizontal floors). In the latter, it is as if the house straddles some sort of force field that has distorted its otherwise orthogonal geometry.

The Raybould House, Connecticut, USA was designed by Kolatan & MacDonald in 1997.

151

INTERLUDE: using a computer to generate complex (mathematically based) forms

Complex geometries can be generated using computers. This is something that is impossible with your blocks; it is something that requires sophisticated resources to achieve in any real materials. It involves the use of computer software to generate complex (generally curved) forms that would be difficult if not impossible to achieve by other means. Whether or not this is 'a good thing' remains a live debate as I write. It can produce sensational buildings. It can be criticised as reducing architecture to sculpture in prioritising sensational three-dimensional form over sensible and poetic building and inhabitation. In today's Building Design *(Friday May 6, 2011) I find (and it saves me having to find more academic substantiation) the following:*

> 'At long last, Frank Gehry famously declared some 20 years ago as he introduced his flamboyant new plasticity, we can, with the aid of the computer, build any form in any shape we can imagine. To which Cedric Price rejoined: why should we build any form or shape we do not need.' (Which is a bit like asking mountaineers why they climb mountains.)

Even in my desktop publishing software there is a menu item labelled 'Pen Tool' with which I can doodle complex curved shapes.

More sophisticated computer software enables the generation of complex forms in three dimensions and can model and dimension the component parts from which such a building could be built (by Building Information Modelling, as mentioned on page 93, using 'parametric'

software, a brief definition of which is given on page 170 of Analysing Architecture*). An example is the extensive 'veil' of structure that shrouds the Yas Marina Hotel (Asymptote Architecture, 2009) at the Abu Dhabi Formula One motor racing circuit.*

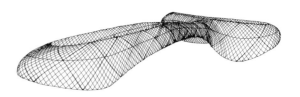

The generation of complex forms by means of computer software is an application of mathematical formulae. As such it might be considered a form of 'ideal geometry'. But it expands the repertoire of mathematically defined form. Fascination with the square, circle, Golden Rectangle... is eclipsed by the ability to produce an infinite variety of forms that emulate the complex curves of a breaking ocean wave, a sea shell, wrinkled fabric, the pseudopodium of an amoeba... It aspires (again) to the apparently geometric authority of nature. But now nature is not seen in terms of circles, squares, Golden Rectangles... but in terms of more complex dynamic formulae: vector, parametric and fractal rather than Euclidean geometries.

The possibilities of computer generated form challenge (or perhaps redefine) the 'geometry of making' in that generally every component piece from which resultant complex curved forms are constructed is different from every other. Rather than using standard parts (such as the brick or rectangular sheet of glass) each has to be made individually and precisely, and carefully labelled so that it can be put in the right position in the jigsaw of the final building.

SUMMARY OF SECTION TWO

Architecture is fundamentally geometric. It involves giving form to parts of the physical world in which we live, making places to fit ourselves and our activities. Geometry conditions how we build. It is through geometry that we strive for perfect form or to emulate nature.

Some of the difficulty in learning how to do architecture derives from the fact that it involves not one but a number of different kinds of geometry. What is more confusing, these different geometries do not always agree with each other. They rarely if ever do, however conscious you are of them, their relative claims to priority, and however hard you try to resolve conflicts. Because these geometries relate to different aspects of architecture - place making; the form of the person; the world; relating things to each other; accommodating social gatherings; assembling building components; composing complex plans; sculptural form... - they each present different issues. The different geometries provoke radically different ways of doing architecture. You can see their relative claims to priority as practical, aesthetic, moral.

You should be conscious of the different kinds of geometry. Decisions can then be made about whether to try to harmonise them, find compromises between them, reconcile them... or perhaps to exploit their conflicts.

In this section we have seen that architecture can involve various kinds of geometry, some of which emerge from how the world works and some that we bring to it from mathematics.

These different geometries include:
- the **circle of place** and its **centre**;
- the **axis** generated by a doorway, which relates to the eyes (line of sight) of the person and which can create a point of focus inside an enclosure or remote, out in the landscape or beyond the horizon;
- the geometries of the **world** and of the **person**, both of which have four sides or directions - north, east, south, west and forward, back, left and right;
- our related propensity for **aligning** things to make them neat and tidy, or to feel that disparate things can be assembled (composed) as an integrated whole;
- **anthropometry** - the geometry of the human body, its dimensions and how it moves;
- **social geometry** - the patterns human beings make when they come together as groups;
- the geometries imposed by the shapes of materials used for building and the ways in which they can be assembled - the **geometry of making**;
- the related geometries of **furniture** and of **planning**, which are related to that of making;
- **ideal geometry** derived from simple mathematical formulae or mechanical

construction – squares, circles, $\sqrt{2}$ rectangles, Golden Rectangles... cubes, spheres, cylinders, prisms...

• **more complex ideal geometries**, which seem to mimic or transcend natural forms and processes – fractures, warps, waves, shells, amoeba...

Put simply (simplistically) these geometries divide into those that reside in the world and our existence in it – geometries of being – and those we try to impose upon the world – ideal geometry. The former includes the geometry of our own body and that by which we interpret our world as well as the geometry that conditions how we build things. The latter includes geometries we construct mathematically and mechanically, whether by ruler and compasses or by using computers.

Some people have made a moral and aesthetic case for following the authority of the geometries of being in doing architecture (even though we have seen that often these are in conflict with each other – as when the circle of place conflicts with the geometry of making). Others claim that it is in the realm of ideal geometry (nowadays using the potential of computers) that human beings can break free of the 'natural' to achieve perfection or novelty, and progressively to transcend what is thought possible.

Only you can decide which of these attitudes to adopt.

There is an obvious kinship between architecture and geometry. Both reside, primarily, in the mind. Architecture manifests the geometries of being. Ideal geometry offers assistance to the architect; it provides ready made forms – the square, the cube, the circle, the cylinder, the sphere... the Golden Rectangle, the $\sqrt{2}$ rectangle... the spiral, the catenary curve... more complex computer-generated forms – that may be applied to a design. But ideal geometry can be seductive, whether because of the apparent 'rightness' of its shapes or the subtlety of computer generated forms that seem to emulate the beautiful forms of nature. The authority ideal geometry seems to possess and the possibilities the computer offers can easily eclipse other considerations in the architect's mind. They offer a realm that transcends the pragmatic, the everyday, even the real. But this is a realm in which it is easy to lose sight of the person, the circle of place, the geometry of making... It is a realm where self-indulgence (on the part of the architect) can usurp consideration for those who will use and live in a building. From being frames for life, buildings can become objects of attention, seen at their best as pieces of sculpture, themselves framed by the rectangle of a photograph.

Now we shall leave board and blocks behind and go out into the world.

OUT INTO THE REAL WORLD

Section Three
OUT INTO THE REAL WORLD

This third set of exercises will take you away from that special isolated little world that was the board on which you built models with your children's wooden blocks. The following exercises ask you to go out into the real world where buildings are generally intended to be and where many other factors come into play.

It is rare for student architects to be able to build their designs. For the most part, throughout schools of architecture, students must work in abstract, producing drawings and models at scales generally smaller than reality. Building is too expensive an activity, beset by regulations and the need for permissions, and dependent on skilled building contractors, to do otherwise. Student painters paint their paintings. Student sculptors sculpt their sculptures. Student writers write their novels. Even student composers can organise their colleagues into an orchestra to perform their music. But it is very hard, generally impossible, for student architects to see their own designs made into real buildings. As the projects set in the school's studio start to become more complex and deal in designs intended to be considered as permanent, the possibility becomes less and less likely. But right at the beginning of a course in architecture, when things remain relatively rudimentary, there is a privileged moment when it is possible to find time to experience the excitement of changing the world (a small part of it at least) by making a real work of architecture, even if it is only temporary and at a modest scale. (Of course this is a privileged moment that may be repeated over and over again throughout your career, each time you go to the beach or out onto the hills... each time you begin to think how to respond to a project.)

EXERCISE 12: making places in the landscape

This exercise has more dimensions and subtleties to it than you might at first think. It introduces many aspects of architecture that remain relevant and retain their potential even in the most sophisticated work. Though intended for the real world, most architecture is designed in abstract through drawings and models (on the drawing table or the computer) but in this exercise you will work in reality, on real sites with real materials, making real places. And that means that you can respond more sensitively (than when working in abstract) to the particularities of the context within which you are working: its topography (the lie of the land, bodies of water, prospects, the horizon...); prevailing conditions (breezes, the sun, ground conditions...); available resources (materials for building, help from others); things that are already there (natural or made by other people, nearby or remote).

Response to and interaction with these particularities enriches architecture. Taking them into account, exploiting them, will prevent your architecture being contained in its own hermetically sealed conceptual world. This does not mean you do not need to bring your own ideas to bear.

EXERCISE 12a. Preparation.

There are lots of things to think about in relation to this exercise. Before you start, bear in mind the following:
- you may go wherever you wish to do these exercises – to the beach, into the woods, out onto the moors, up trees or rock faces... or just into your back garden or yard; (wherever you go, make sure you are not trespassing on someone else's property; ask permission if you need to); if you cannot go anywhere, try doing the exercise in your imagination (after all, that's where architecture primarily happens) but it is better to work with a real situation, real conditions, real materials;
- an early decision in any architectural project (except when a site is predetermined and constricted) is to decide on the location of your place – in open space, under a tree, against a rock or wall, beside a stream...; this involves recognising potential; your decision on location will have important consequences, possibilities as well as problems; think about how your place will relate to its context, benefiting from views, shelter, support, defined access (i.e. a controllable way in and out)...;
- think carefully and imaginatively about how you might use things that are already there (not that you necessarily *have* to, but it would be a shame to miss an

opportunity); you might be able to use that
tree for shade, that rock as an anchor for
your place or as a seat or altar, that
wall as a support for a sheltering roof,
the stream for water and for cooling your
feet...;

• another important early decision is to
decide on the intended content of your
new place – the brief (program) for your
project; will it be for your own occupation
or do you want it to accommodate a specific
'possession' (your dog, partner, a work of
art, a 'god' of some sort...) or frame a
particular activity (cooking and eating a
meal, playing a game, performing some sort
of ceremony or ritual, telling a story,
singing, canoodling...)?; maybe it will
be no more than a place to sit and look
out to sea; remember, the possibility of
occupation is essential to place making;

• you may use any materials available (so
long as you do not cause criminal damage,
kill living trees or, without permission,
take anything that belongs to someone
else); if you wish you might also take some
ready-made components with you – string,
rope, a blanket or beach towel, a windbreak, a small tent...; you might decide to
make a place using only materials you find
at your location;

• you may also take tools with you; if you
had the use of a mechanical excavator then
you would be able to dig bigger holes than
with your bare hands(!)... but generally

speaking a knife and small spade should be
sufficient; remember that this project is
not about doing irreversible damage;

• place-making can involve taking away
as well as adding, excavation as well as
construction; it might involve digging a
shallow pit in the sand or clearing the
ground of twigs and stones;

• your task is to make a real place, *not*
a model of one (such as a sand castle,
a sand dolls house, or a sand motorway
interchange...);

• be neither too ambitious nor too modest
in your aspiration; some of the most
powerful places in the landscape are
simple – a standing stone or a circle of
them, a cave, a platform at the edge of a
precipice, the shade of a tree...; quality
is not a direct corollary of complexity;
if you want to make simple places that do
not involve much time then make a number
of them; but also take time to reflect
on their power in the landscape; think
about what they do for and to you as their
occupant and perpetrator;

• think about what you are going to do
before you start (this is called 'having an
idea', and remember that architecture is
about having ideas); but also be prepared
to modify your idea (for the better) in
response to things that happen or impinge
on your place as you make it;

• making places always depends on ideas;
you have to provide those; no one knows

where ideas might come from (often they come from your memory, which needs constantly to be restocked) but as an architect they are your primary, and essential, stock in trade;

• enjoy the power (and thrill) of changing the world (hopefully for the better!);

• afterwards, it would probably be best to remove your place and return the land to how it was; but if you do not have to do this straight away, watch how others respond to your place, maybe using it (as you intended?), maybe skirting around it suspicious of its powers, maybe adapting it, maybe destroying it...;

• reflect on your own feelings when dismantling your place (I was once told of a scout who wept when the camp in which he had lived for a week was struck); sometimes, with devilment, we delight in destroying a place, perhaps wanting to deny others the enjoyment of it or to wipe away the guilt of a hubristic affront to the world (though having the audacity to change the world is essential to being an architect).

What you could learn

The chief aim of this task is to ask your imagination to engage in the primary purpose of all architecture: to identify place. It asks you to do this in reality (rather than in abstract or through the medium of drawing or modelling). It prompts you to make real (if temporary) works of architecture. This is made possible by asking you to do it in a temporary way, on common or freely available land using materials ready to hand; that is, it does not require formal permissions and will not be prohibitively expensive. It involves response to real conditions: the sun, weather, topography (the lie of the land), the horizon, existing features in the landscape, and other creatures (including other people). This exercise also asks you to think carefully about how your place accommodates its content: the person, possessions, activity, mood... it will frame.

Even though the exercise may lean towards the production of relatively small scale places established using unsophisticated construction it nevertheless allows exploration of many of the subtle dimensions and factors that come into play in architecture.

159

EXERCISE 12b. Identify a place by choice and occupation.

At its most rudimentary, doing architecture need not involve building anything at all. Architecture begins with occupation. You identify a place just by being there.

Wherever you are, out in the landscape, survey your surroundings and choose a place to put yourself.

If you find it difficult to decide where to put yourself, one way is to use chance (which has been used in decisions about place-making since ancient times) – chance might include throwing something and seeing where it lands, watching to see where a particular bird perches, watching a toddler walking along and seeing where it falls down... and then making your place there. Doing this, chance will make your decision for you but it will also set you challenges (especially if that bird perches high in a tree or half way up a cliff, or settles out at sea, or that toddler stumbles in a rock pool); you must however stick to your principle of following chance.

Alternatively, you might take care in deciding where to put yourself, analysing the advantages and disadvantages of a range of possibilities. While doing this, allow ideas to arise in your mind about what you might do in this place even if it is only to sit and read a book; though you might equally choose it as a place to count passers-by or to perform some sort of ceremony; you might want it as a place to lay ambush to a friend or to have an intimate conversation.

Wherever you choose, the activity you will perform (however passive) will (should) influence your choice; different activities require different circumstances.

In doing this task, you are doing something you have done unselfconsciously many times before; but this time be conscious of what you are doing and how you are making your decisions.

Do not, for the moment, modify your place in any way; though you might begin to think how you might add or take away something to make it more comfortable or to enable you to perform your chosen activity more effectively. You have already begun to do architecture just by choosing your place, weighing up factors that influence your decision. Beginning to think about how you might modify it takes you to the second stage of doing architecture (often thought of as the first) – i.e. having ideas about how you might physically change the world (a small part of it) according to needs and desires.

IN YOUR NOTEBOOK...

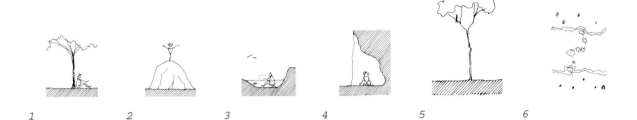

1   2   3   4   5   6

**In your notebook... draw examples (from
experience, memory and imagination) of
places identified by choice and occupation.**

At some time of your life you have probably
sat in the shade under a tree (1). You have
probably also stood on the highest point
of a rock, maybe chanting 'I'm the king of
the castle!' (2). You might have sat in a
rock pool splashing in the water (3) or
nestled into a cave to shelter from rain
and wind or hide from friends (4). Perhaps
you have climbed to a high branch to survey
the land around or just out of bravado
(5), or carefully threaded a path stepping
from rock to rock across a stream (6).
These are all examples of identifying place
by choice and occupation. They are all
examples of you exercising your capacity
for architecture at its most rudimentary.

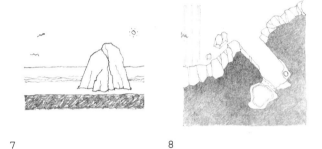

7   8

You would be satisfying Exercise 12b by
doing any of the above but perhaps there
are other opportunities. Maybe you just
want to settle adjacent to a rock that has
presence in the landscape (7), feeling its
companionship or using it as an anchor
– i.e. next to it you feel you are in a
specific place, not just floating in the
anywhere. You might hide in crevice in a
rock face to get out of sight of others
(8). You might find two rocks you can sit
between (9), or two trees that make a
doorway (10). You might find a clearing
in the woods (11) that feels like a room.

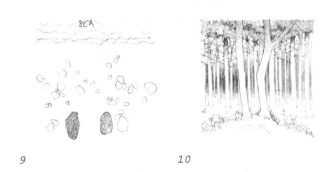

9   10

11

You do not need to do anything to these. As soon as you see them (recognise them as places) and then occupy them (even if only in your mind) they become places. They can all be the seeds from which more developed and more permanent architecture can grow.

You might want to find a place where you can perform. The theatre director Peter Brook and his company have put on performances in informal venues around the world. He describes how these are chosen:

'With a simple pragmatism (which is the basis of everything) we would look around and see that in one place there are some nice trees or a tree where the villagers normally gather; or there'd be another place that's exposed with a breeze. In one place the soil is bumpy; in another it's flat. In one place there's a little clearing with earth that rises to the sides in a natural amphitheatre so more people can see... Spatially speaking, one is here touching on things that every architect should experience for himself, which is finding what is conducive; this conducts and that doesn't.'

Peter Brook, quoted in Andrew Todd and Jean-Guy Lecat – *The Open Circle*, 2003, pp. 49-50.

Sensitivity to the 'conducive' has been part of people's response to and relationship with the landscape since ancient times. Locations such as Dunino Den in Scotland have been used for sacred ceremonies possibly for hundreds or even thousands of years. Its topography is theatrical. There is a rocky promontory in a wooded river gorge.

section

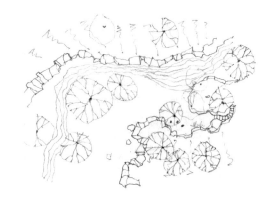

plan

You can imagine ceremonies being conducted on the top of the promontory and witnessed by people standing on the bank of the river below.

162

Prospect and refuge; refuge and arena

In his book *The Experience of Landscape* (1975, page 58) Jay Appleton quotes the Austrian zoologist Konrad Lorenz:

> *'We are taking a walk in the forest... We approach a forest glade... We now tread slowly and more carefully. Before we break through the last bushes and out of cover on to the free expanse of the meadow, we do what all wild animals and all good naturalists, wild boars, leopards, hunters and zoologists would do under similar circumstances: we reconnoitre, seeking, before we leave our cover, to gain from it the advantage which it can offer alike to hunter and hunted – namely to see without being seen.'*

You might consider this when selecting your place. Sitting in woods beside a lake...

... you are hidden but can watch what happens on the arena of the water.

Sitting in a cave you have the security of your refuge and the advantage of a prospect, so you can seen anyone, enemy or friend, approaching.

It is as if your relationship with place is an expansion of the relationship between the inside of your head and the world.

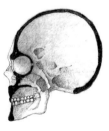

The place you choose to occupy in the landscape is like an extra skull, into which you can withdraw for protection. Its doorway or window is your eyes.

Relationship with the horizon, ground surface

In assessing and choosing your place you might also like to consider this:

'My interest has always been where to put man in relation to the horizon' (the ground surface) *'in a built environment... Everything we build must be adjusted in relation to the ground, thus the horizon becomes an important aspect of architecture... Where between heaven and earth do I place people?'*

> Sverre Fehn, quoted and translated in Fjeld – Sverre Fehn: *The Pattern of Thoughts*, 2009, pp.108-110

Places have very different characters and potentials depending on their relationship with the surface of the ground.

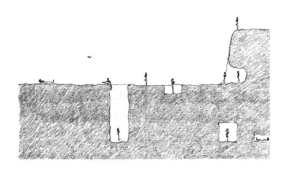

Give thought to the different relationship with the landscape you have if you are on top of a cliff, in a cave, underground... from if you are standing on a level plane.

Mere use

Places may be made merely by use. Sheep crossing hillsides (or cats lawns) make pathways. Men striking matches on doorjambs, to light their pipes, left black slashes of sulphur on the stone. A patch of blood on a pavement marks the scene of a murder. The fingers of countless pilgrims polish the toe of a saint. In a film about his origins, the artist Miroslav Balka shows a small patch of worn floor in his grandmother's house. It is where she knelt to pray every day. Balka calls it a 'trace'. It was his grandmother's chapel and is now her shrine. The film is at: http://channel.tate.org.uk/media/47872674001 *(June 2010)*. Places are receptacles of memory. Place and meaning, place and memory, are intertwined. Places speak of the intimate relationship between the person and the world occupied.

INTERLUDE: Uluru (Ayer's Rock)

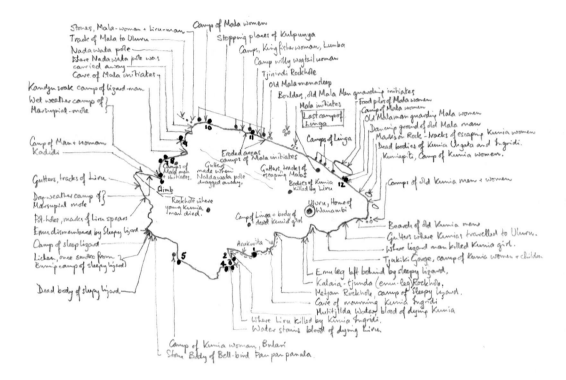

Ascribing meaning to places in the landscape is essential to the way we make sense of the world in which we live. We choose places to sit, to hide, to sleep... according to criteria of comfort, shelter, security... Such places also acquire meaning through memory. On revisiting a beach we might remember the particular rock on which we sat warming in the sun or the cave in which we hid when playing 'hide-and-seek'. Places might acquire meaning through association with history – that is where so and so made that speech, was assassinated, killed in a air crash... – or with myth.

Traditional Australian aborigine culture has an intimate relationship with the landscape. It constructs little in the way of built architecture. The architecture it does make consists almost wholly of ascribing meaning to specific places in the landscape. At Uluru (Ayer's Rock) for example there are hundreds of specific places each of which is associated with a particular mythical event. (Some of them are

noted in the drawing above.) This ascription of meanings to places makes this massive red rock the aborigine equivalent of one of the great cathedrals of Europe.

Traditional aborigine culture makes sense of the wider landscape in similar ways. By the memory of 'songlines' spun in the indeterminate past aborigine people tell stories of mythological events in the Dreamtime. These hold the landscape together and make sense of it for generation after generation.

Each of us does the same sort of thing in the neighbourhood where we live, where we grew up... We can each tell stories which involve specific places and spin into stories that superimpose a personal map of sense on the bare physical environment. Such maps of sense, whether personal or cultural, are important in architecture. They are significant manifestations of architecture in that they derive from our capacity, and existential need, to identify place.

1

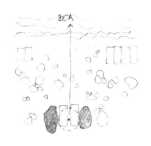

2

EXERCISE 12c. (Begin to) make your place better in some way.

You have selected a spot that you recognise as a place. Maybe you can inhabit it, occupy it and in some (maybe slight) way feel 'at home' in it. Now do something to it that will make it better, more in accord with your practical needs, or more interesting, engaging or beautiful.

You might set up camp with chairs, towels and perhaps a wind break in or at the mouth of the crevice in the rocks (1) identifying with it as a place and implying that, like a snail with its shell, you might withdraw into it for security (or just to change into your swimming costume).

You might line the ground between the twin rocks with towels to make it more comfortable and plant a parasol to shade you from the sun (2). By doing so you have made yourself a small house using the parallel walls of the stones.

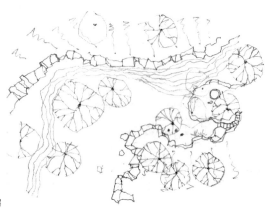

On a cool evening you might build a fire in the centre of the rocky clearing (3). It becomes a place to cook food and talk or sing songs.

At Dunino Den (4) a circular basin was carefully cut into the top of rocky promontory. This was presumably to be used in the performance of rituals, maybe baptisms. Alongside the basin is carved what appears to be a footprint. Maybe this was where the officiating priest stood.

3

4

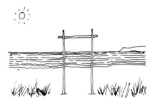

Other senses

You can intervene in other ways than by physically changing the fabric of the landscape. You might identify your place, for example, with sound. The Norwegian architect Sverre Fehn wrote:

> 'Once I visited Greece and during the day I sat under a tree' (i.e. Fehn making his own place in the landscape) 'I studied a shepherd and his flock.' (i.e. refuge and arena) 'I thought, Here is a person who walks in the landscape with his sound. He finds sound constructions with his whistle. The man with the instrument had a sound dialogue with the landscape. The shepherd found his own theater in the landscape.'

> Sverre Fehn, quoted and translated in Fjeld – Sverre Fehn: *The Pattern of Thoughts*, 2009, p.15

Fehn went on to evoke the sound of a church bell (and presumably he could have also cited the *muezzin* calling the faithful to prayer at a mosque) drawing attention to its architectural power in identifying place (associating it with a particular religion or event).

You can also identify a place with smell (or perfume). You can imagine situations where smell is an important ingredient in the character of a place.

I have run this place-making exercise as a student project in various schools of architecture. On one occasion some students made their place by constructing a simple doorway of three sticks at the highest point of a sand dune.

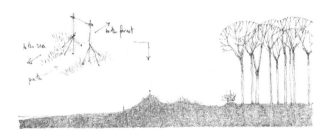

Approaching it from inland it identified the place at which they first saw a full view of the expanse of sea (top). Approaching in the other direction, from the beach, it was the point at which they first became aware of the perfume of the pine forest. The doorway identified the place of an affecting threshold. It marked it and framed it with an elemental work of architecture.

EXERCISE 12d. Making a new place on open ground.

You identify place by yourself too, without building on what is already there. A beach is like a pristine blank canvas. Standing on an open beach, like the monk in Caspar David Friedrich's painting, 'The Monk by the Sea', 1808-10,...

You stand there as the seed from which a building (a temple or a house) might grow. The direction in which you face could become the direction your temple or house would face (above). The building would mediate between you and your surroundings; it would also represent your presence and geometry.

Dancing on the beach...

... you identify a place. And with your own directions (the geometry of your body) you begin to give that place architecture.

... you establish your own dance floor (its limits will be marked by your footprints). That place is the forerunner of the *orkestra* (the dancing floor of the ancient Greek theatre, set in the landscape). It invokes the powerful relationship between people, activity and landscape.

Lying on the ground you make a bed.

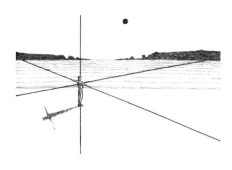

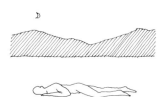

INTERLUDE: Richard Long

The artist Richard Long has made many places in landscapes around the world. You can see some photographs of his work at:
www.richardlong.org/sculptures/sculptures.html *(May 2011)*

He has made pathways merely by walking repeatedly along a line. As he does, his feet wear the grass or compact the dust under him leaving a trace of his walking.

The results are tangible memories of his having been there, treading a particular line over and over again. (Because they will gradually disappear, he records them in photographs.) These pathways are also reminiscent of the pathways worn by sheep as they wander repeatedly along the same routes along the side of a hill.) Long has also made circles in the same way, by walking around and around, consistently on the same line.

Sometimes he makes lines or circles with found stones or pieces of timber, imposing on them a (nearly) perfect geometry that only a mind could provide.

Sometimes he makes a line or circle merely by the removal of stones, to clear a path or a performance place.

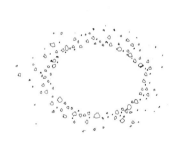

Some of his sculptures seem to identify place; other to deny it. (The denial of place is an architectural act too.)

He has also identified place, created tangible memories, with his body. On a showery day he will look for a large flat rock. Lying on it, he waits for the rain. As it falls he lies motionless. When it stops he stands up to photograph the dry patch (the rain shadow) left on the rock in the shape of his body...

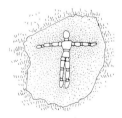 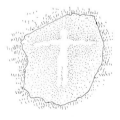

... a 'home' vacated by its inhabitant.

EXERCISE 12e. Circle of place.

Draw a circle of place about yourself.

_____

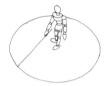

You did this with your small person on your board; but now feel the power of a circle of place that you can inhabit. Sense the way the circle frames you and separates you from the world around. Be aware of the threshold it creates between inside and outside. Step over the threshold. Stand on the outside and consider the power of the circle in the wider landscape. Persuade yourself that inside the circle is a special, even magical, place, where strange things might happen to you. (It is: the circle singles you out as special when you stand inside it.) Steel yourself to step back inside. Feel the slight frisson as you step over the line. All these effects are part of the fundamental emotional dimensions of all architecture

based in identification of place. However sophisticated architecture might get, it begins with this rudimentary separation of an inside from everywhere else. This is so even if the dividing line, the threshold, is not so clear as your line in the sand.

By drawing your circle you have identified a place that did not exist before. (In a small but significant way, you have changed the world.) Though it is no more than a line in the sand it persists. It continues to represent your presence even when you leave it. It is the most rudimentary form your 'home' might take. To make it a proper home you would have to do more; but this is where it starts.

Separation - distinguishing a place from its surroundings - does not always happen on land. In 2008 there were severe floods in the Bihar region of India. People who had lost their homes made sleeping platforms in the water. They shaded them from the sun with roofs that would also shed further rain.

EXERCISE 12f. (Begin to) modify your circle of place (to make it stronger or more comfortable).

Starting with your circle of place, think how you might make it stronger as a place in itself, more comfortable (commodious) as a place to live, or more attuned to another purpose (perhaps as a place to display an object or perform a ceremony of some sort). Use whatever materials you have to hand: stones; driftwood; grass; the sand (or earth) itself; even other people.

Notice, while you are doing this, that beginning with the idea of the circle of place leads you into a different way of thinking of your building from if you begin with the thought that you are making a building as an object (a sculptural object). Forms that begin with the circle of place are concerned with *framing* (the person, an object, an activity...) rather than *being* framed (as in a photograph or drawing). Consequently, the person is treated as an ingredient of architecture rather than as a spectator of it. You can think later about what your building looks like; think first about what your building does to and for the person.

Marker or focus

You might begin by erecting something to stand vertical as a focus and marker of the place. It could be a piece of driftwood...

... or a stone (make it as large a stone as you can manage).

You might place a large flat stone as an altar, a table or a grave.

You might make a hearth with a fire. It defines a circle (with no clear threshold) of heat and light.

Or you might plant a tree (which will take time to grow).

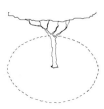

Each will generate its own circle of place (presence). The tree defines its circle with its canopy of branches, making a place you can occupy.

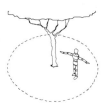

Each also generates (at least) two other circles: the intimate circle within which you can touch (or tend or hug) the marker...

... and the extensive circle of visibility, within which you can see the marker.

Performance place

Next make circles in which you can occupy the centre. Try outlining your circle with stones. You can stand at the centre; you can be the focus of the circle.

The circle also becomes a space open for performance; a space for make-believe and ritual.

which makes possible axial linkage with the remote.

Doorways and axes

With your stone circle, you can also experiment, as you did with your blocks on the board, with making a doorway as a specific point at which to cross the threshold between outside and inside...

Try different permutations. Enjoy the power of setting down a spatial matrix, an architectural composition of elements, that organises your sense of the world around you and your relationship with it.

Temple, church, mosque...

... a doorway that generates an axis. Which can establish a link with something remote, such as a distant mountain or the rising (or setting) sun.

You can play with combinations of focus, circle of place, yourself, and the doorway

In doing this you will have effectively built a temple, a church or a mosque, depending on the arrangement of elements you have chosen to make. You have made a real work of architecture in the real world to which you can relate in a real way. A church, for example, makes a circle of place (though it may be cruciform in plan) around an altar.

Its steeple acts as a marker that can be seen from a distance.

The church's west doorway (and its orientation) establishes a link with the east (and the rising sun) and aligns it with the cardinal directions of the world.

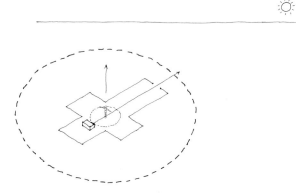

And if you build (or just imagine) a spire that straddles the church's circle of place then you have also indicated the vertical direction – the *axis mundi* (axis of the world) – that stretches into the sky (up to heaven). The steeple (marker) then generates its own circle of place (shown dotted) which might be identified by the wall of the churchyard, within the sanctified ground of which the dead are buried, as if to be protected by a

shield, a force field generated by the church and its altar. Whatever its style or ornamentation, a church is a composition of the basic architectural elements of focus (altar), circle(s) of place, marker, doorway and its axis, and the person. It is a composition that has the effect of giving form not only to its specific place but also to an interpretation of the world around it. It gives the person a place to relate to; it makes sense of the world.

You might, alternatively, make a small temple to yourself.

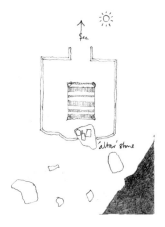

In this example someone has chosen a particular rock on the beach as an altar. Adjacent to this they outlined the walls of a small temple with a doorway, the axis of which established a link from the 'altar' to the horizon over the sea. Inside this small temple they laid their towel, like the catafalque in a crematorium chapel.

Exercise 12g. Making places with people.

Try making architecture using your friends as your material for building. A line of people can be a wall (like the defensive line in a game of football).

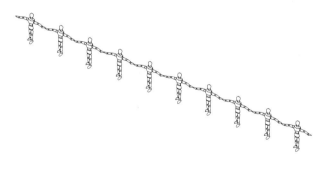

Just before the wall between West and East Berlin was built in the 1960s its position was identified (defended) by a line of Russian soldiers, who themselves constituted a wall dividing West from East.

Use two of your friends to make a doorway.

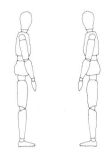

Walk through it. Be sensitive to that frisson as you pass between then.

In 1977, Marina Abramovic and her partner Ulay stood naked in the entrance to one of their exhibitions. (It was titled 'Imponderabilia'.) Visitors had to squeeze between them, choosing which to face as they did.

If you have sufficient friends, arrange them to line a pathway, like a guard of honour leading to the doorway of a church at a funeral or the wedding of a soldier.

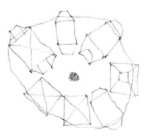

Arrange your friends in a circle (a precursor of the circle of standing stones) to identify a place within which some shared activity (a ritual, a play, a fight...) might happen.

Or they might face outwards as a defensive formation; as when soldiers formed themselves into squares, or pioneers

circled their wagons, to defend against attack.

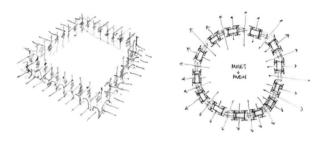

You could make these social geometries more permanent by building them in physical form. A defensive formation would become a fortress of some kind; a guard of honour might be made more permanent by planting an arcade of trees or erecting two parallel lines of standard lamps.

A circle of people may become a circle of their tents or houses. The circle of people can become the houses around a market square or village green.

'*Late in the afternoon they started to build a sand castle near the water's edge... The walls had to be squared off, there had to be windows, shells were to be embedded at regular intervals and the area inside the keep had to be made comfortable with dry seaweed... When everything was completed and they had walked around their achievement several times, they squeezed inside the walls and sat down to wait for the tide. Kate was convinced that their castle was so well built it could resist the sea. Stephen and Julie went along with this, deriding the water when it simply lapped around the sides, booing it when it sucked away a piece of wall.'*

Ian McEwan - A Child in Time, 1987.

In this example some children have built (moulded) a place to sit together and talk.

...or a medieval chapter house.

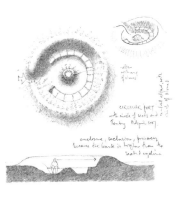

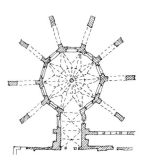

They have scooped sand to make a depression in the beach, deepening that depression by mounding the sand into a circular bank around it. They have left a doorway oriented towards the sea. The wall is high enough to conceal the occupants from the rest of the beach and to make the place feel enclosed when sitting inside. Around the base of the wall, inside, the children have formed a bench seat divided into individual places. At the centre, where there might have been a hearth, they have built an altar decorated with stones. It is a manifestation of the same architectural idea (based in social geometry) as an iron age house (see Case Study 1 in *Analysing Architecture*, 3rd edition)...

Playing with combinations of focus, circle of place, the doorway and its axis, and your self (and friends) is a matter of bringing those ideas you explored with your blocks out into the world, out from the conceptual realm of your mind (and the arena of the board or drawing board) into reality. This process is essential to architecture, which originates in the mind but, when realised, changes the real world. You might continue playing with the ideas you explored with your blocks in the early exercises of this book.

INTERLUDE: Australian aborigine place making in the landscape

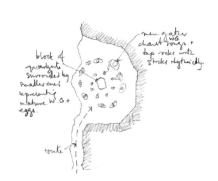

1

The traditional architecture of Australian aborigine tribes consists mainly of place making in the landscape. (Most of the following examples are taken from Spencer and Gillen, Native Tribes of Central Australia, 1898.)

The aborigine way of making sense of their world by the spinning of 'songlines' that tie places in the landscape together in a net of stories has already been mentioned (on page 165). Distinctive pieces of landscape are associated with particular myths. Emily Gap, for example, is the cult site of the Witchetty Grub tribe. The general landscape there, which is the trace of a creek through a gorge, is invested with meaning as a route followed by the ancestors. Many stories are each associated with their own specific features in the arrangement of rocks, trees, caves... The ancestral route leads to a sacred cave in the side of the gorge (1). There ceremonies are performed in a circle around a quartzite altar representing a witchetty grub. The circle is formed by smaller rocks representing the eggs of the grub. During the ritual, men from the tribe form a further circle outside this, where they rhythmically strike rocks together.

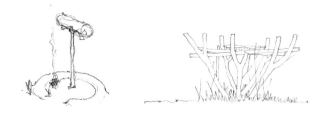

2

All ceremonies require arenas on which to be performed. Areas of ground are swept clean of rocks and scrub, leaving a curb of debris to mark the threshold between inside and out (2). Such arenas are not always circular. Various markers set out the court on which the ceremony is to be performed, indicating where particular things happen. The people not performing – the rest of the tribe, the audience – stand outside the threshold.

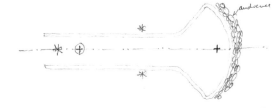

3

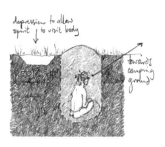

4

Markers and platforms are erected to support, display and honour remains or other sacred objects (3 and 4). Some are set in their own small circles of place.

Graves are dug in which the dead are interred (5) sitting up and facing the tribe's camping ground, and provided with a symbolic access 'hatch' for the spirit, in the form of a depression in the ground alongside.

5

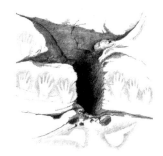

1

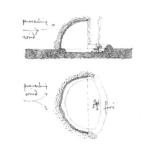

2

As may be seen on page 69 of Analysing Architecture *(3rd edition), small crevices in rock faces might be used as graves (1), marked with the hand stencils of relatives.*

Sacred totems, moulded from the earth and decorated with pigment, are screened within circles of brush (2). This drawing shows, in plan and section, the representation - the embodiment - of a snake god.

3

Small shelters are built to protect a fire from the prevailing breeze and to make a sheltered place to sit (3). Shelters might be built to separate an initiate from the world for a period before undergoing some ritual.

Walls might be built of brush to screen a ritual ceremony - such as the circumcision of a boy - from the rest of the tribe (4). Once the ceremony has been performed, at a sacred pole, the brush wall is broken open to make a doorway through which the boy returns to the tribe as an adult.

Other tribes make an altar formed of the male relatives of a boy (5). This is the table on which the operation is performed.

4

All these are examples of the human impetus for place making, which is the seed of all architecture. Places, whether identified just by use, formed of people themselves, or modified by building are essential to the functioning of any culture. In your own way you can experiment with all of these aborigine places yourself, making places in the landscape, recognising the potential of places that are already there, making new places, clearing ground, using other people, defining circles of place, erecting markers, platforms, shelters... You can experience the power of such places to affect your perception of the world, your place in it, and even your own identity.

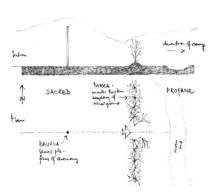

5

INTERLUDE: Ettore Sottsass

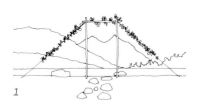

1

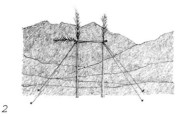

2

3

In the 1970s the designer Ettore Sottsass played with making places in the landscape. In some he put the doorway at the centre of the circle of place, putting a threshold - a point of transition - at the focus of attention.

4

He made, for example, a 'Doorway through which you will meet your love' (1), which framed a view of a mountain across a lake and had a rocky path leading to it. He also made a 'Doorway through which to enter into darkness' (2) and another 'Doorway through which you may not pass' (3). Such doorways in the landscape are redolent of traditional Japanese Shinto gateways (4). They stand as visible objects but our relationship with them is that they prompt the idea in our minds of what it would be like to pass through them and what we would find or experience when we did.

As well as doorways, Sottsass made other elemental places the subjects of which were the person in the landscape. For example, he laid out blankets and a pillow as an inviting bed in the middle of a grassy meadow (5). He entitled it 'Do you want to sleep...?'.

Sottsass also recognised the potential of places recognised as already there in the landscape. By erecting a banner on a boulder, and providing it with a staircase, he turned the boulder into a place with an indeterminate identity (6). His transformation of existing features in the landscape into places is again redolent of the way in which, in traditional Japanese religion, distinctive landscape features can be developed into shrines (7).

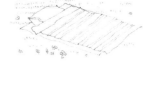

5

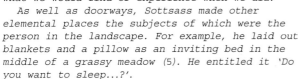

6

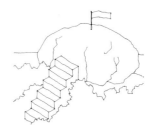

7

180

1

Exercise 12h. Anthropometry.

Experiment with how the size and mobility of your own body influence your occupation, movement through, and making of places in the landscape.

2

Think about how, for example, you choose a place to sit in the landscape. Do you choose a rock between a particular range of heights (1)? Do you choose somewhere where there is something to lean against, a tree trunk (2)? Do you shiggle your bottom into the soft sand of a dune (3) to form a more comfortable seat in the sand, leaving an impression (4) that establishes a 'throne' to which you might return?

3   4

Climb a slope (5), being conscious of how you place your feet and the impressions you leave in the sand. Form steps in the sand (6), maybe with pieces of driftwood, and experiment with different heights for each step. Judge which heights provide the most comfortable experience of climbing the steps. Make notes in your notebook.

5   6

Walk, being aware of the footprints you leave and the spaces between them (7) and how they begin to establish a pathway.

Make doorways of different heights and widths (8), including ones that are too big and too small. Be sensitive to how the different sized doorways make you feel as you go through them. Measure and record the different sizes and your responses in your notebook.

7   8

1

Exercise 12i. Geometry of making.

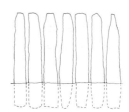

2

Experiment with making architectural
elements – walls, platforms, pits, roofs,
pathways, markers... – using the materials
to hand where you are. (Remember that
architectural elements are the means
by which places for occupation are
identified.)

3

   You can make architectural elements by
digging, mounding and moulding... as when
you dig a pit on the beach mounding the
sand into a wall around your place (1).

   You can make architectural elements by
planting... as when you plant stakes or
stones in the ground (2).

   You can make architectural elements by
weaving... as when you weave twigs together
to make wattle (3).

4

   You can make architectural elements
by leaning... as when you lean branches
together to make a tipi (4).

   You can make architectural elements by
assembling... as when you cut branches and
assemble them into a structure (5).

   You can make architectural elements by
building... as when you put stones on top
of each other to build a wall. In this the

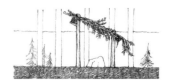

5

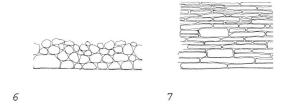

6   7

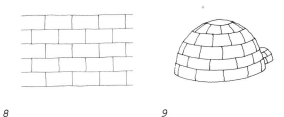

8   9

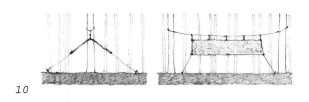

10

11

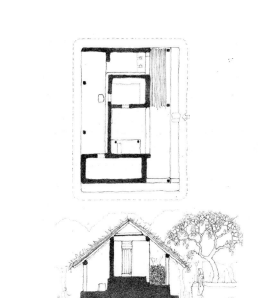

12

form of your wall will be influenced by the characteristics of the stones with which you try to build. You might have to balance pebbles awkwardly on each other (6) or be lucky to find flat stones that balance quite well in courses (7). Trying to build a wall with stones found in the landscape will make you more aware of the benefits of using standard rectangular blocks (8, as you did in the early exercises of this book). If you are in a snowfield you can of course cut your blocks to the shapes you need to make an igloo (9).

You can make architectural elements by supporting, stretching, suspending... as when you stretch a rope between two trees to support a piece of fabric as a shelter or shade (10).

A Mongolian yurt is made by weaving slats of wood (11).

This small house in Kerala is built by mounding and moulding mud, assembling a roof structure, and weaving a roof of coconut leaves (12).

Even more sophisticated buildings are conditioned by the geometries of these various kinds of making... as you will have found when you collected examples in your notebook ('In your notebook...', page 76).

Exercise 12j. Responding to conditions.

When you were making models with your blocks on your board you did not take into account real conditions affecting your place making. You could concern yourself with form in a little world away from sunshine, rain, wind, temperature and the presence of real people.

When you start making places in real conditions you could continue to behave as if you were in that separate little world and ignore sun, rain, wind, air temperature, ground conditions and the presence of other people. Or you can start to think about how your place making might exploit and mitigate the influence of these factors. You can start to think about how you might shelter yourself from excessive sun, from rain that soaks you, from wind that chills you... how you might make yourself warm in cold conditions, how you might make yourself cool in hot conditions... how you might cope with soft or bumpy ground conditions... how you might either give yourself some privacy (in your place) or how you might draw more attention to yourself and make yourself more visible to other people.

Place-making in the landscape is often described and discussed in terms of shelter and survival. In Britain, television adventurers such as Ray Mears demonstrate

in their programmes various ways to make bivouacs in different circumstances as defences against the factors listed above. Even though the places you make will be necessarily rudimentary, these are the same factors addressed by buildings through all history, and even by the most sophisticated and most advanced buildings of today. But you can make yourself aware of the principles of the exploitation and mitigation of conditions by making small places using simple materials in the landscape.

In doing this exercise the first thing to do is to assess the conditions within which you wish to make a place. Are there factors you wish to mitigate? Are there factors you can exploit? Such assessments might (should) influence the specific spot you decide to build. In a cool climate, you might for example choose a more sheltered location or one that is facing the sun. In a hot climate you might look for somewhere that is shaded by trees or open to a prevailing breeze.

Here are some examples of what you might try. Remember that the principal factors to be exploited or mitigated are sun, rain, wind, air temperature, ground conditions and the presence of other people.

Persistent wind is wearing and can chill the body. Animals on hillsides find pockets of space sheltered from biting winds. People can do this too, but we can also

make windbreaks. On the beach you might dig a hole beside a large piece of driftwood (a tree trunk) to make a pocket of still air where you can escape from the wind.

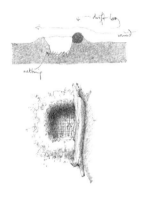

You might have brought a fabric windbreak with you to the beach, beside which you can sit sheltered from the breeze.

Experiment with how far the beneficial effects of the windbreak extend. How big is the pocket of still air it shelters? How near to it do you need to sit to be out of the breeze?

Consider too how the windbreak relates to other factors such as the sun and other people.

According to the position of the sun (above), you could find yourself sitting sheltered from the breeze in full sun or in shade. These create different circumstances.

You might welcome the partial privacy that the windbreak provides and decide to put another on your other side (even though the wind is not blowing from that direction) to screen you from neighbours.

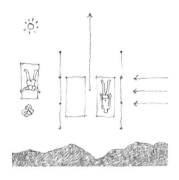

Notice how, in the above sketch, these two simple windbreaks do more than just shelter a place from breeze and from the eyes of other people. Positioned as they are, the cliff behind protects the rear; and together they establish an axis that orientates the place towards the sea. These two windbreaks, promoted to permanent walls, could easily become a temple or a house.

Alternatively, if you are in hot and humid conditions, you might want to open your place to the breeze whilst shading it from the sun.

In cold and wet conditions you will probably want to shelter yourself from both the rain and the wind.

You might also feel the need for a fire to keep yourself warm and dry. You might build your place to capture the heat from a hearth...

You might just want to get out of the sun.

... or to enclose it completely...

You might want to shelter yourself from rain whilst opening your place to cooling breezes.

... though you will need to consider where the smoke from the fire will go.

You might have to deal with ground conditions too. On boggy ground (if you cannot find a drier place to make your place) you might build a base of logs on which to build your shelter.

You might surround your place with a stockade of spiny branches, establishing for yourself a circle of place into which threats may not enter.

Or if you need to make a place when your landscape is flooded, then you might have to build a platform (as the people of Bihar had to in the floods of 2008).

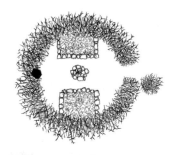

Notice how these simple structures also conform to the geometry of making.

You might want to protect yourself, not so much from the eyes of other people, but the attentions of predatory animals.

This is the sort of camp Masai huntsmen make from spiky branches to protect themselves from animals over night. Notice how it is anchored to a tree, and has a hearth as the centre of its circle of place. A clump of branches closes the doorway and completes the circle of protection.

INTERLUDE: Nick's camp

*In his short story 'Big Two-Hearted River'
Ernest Hemingway describes the making of an
overnight camp:*

'The ground rose, wooded and sandy, to
overlook the meadow, the stretch of river and
the swamp. Nick dropped his pack and rod case
and looked for a level piece of ground. He
was very hungry and wanted to make his camp
before he cooked. Between two jack pines the
ground was quite level. He took the ax out of
the pack and chopped out two projecting roots.
That leveled a piece of ground large enough
to sleep on. He smoothed out the sandy soil
with his hand and pulled all the sweet fern
bushes by their roots. His hands smelled good
from the sweet fern. He smoothed the uprooted
earth. He didn't want anything making lumps
under the blankets. One he folded double, next
to the ground. The other two he spread on
top. With his ax he slit off a bright slab of
pine from one of the big stumps and split it
into pegs for the tent. He wanted them long
and solid to hold in the ground. With the
tent unpacked and spread on the ground, the
pack, leaning against a jack pine, looked much
smaller. Nick tied the rope that served the
tent for a ridge-pole to the trunk of one of
the pine trees and pulled the tent up off the
ground with the other end of the rope and tied
it to the other pine. The tent hung on the
rope like a canvas blanket on a clothesline.
Nick poked a pole he had cut up under the
back peak of the canvas and then made it a
tent by pegging out the sides. He pegged the
sides taut and drove the pegs deep, hitting
them down into the ground with the flat of
the ax until the rope loops were buried and
the canvas was drum tight. Across the open
mouth of the tent Nick fixed cheesecloth to
keep out mosquitoes. He crawled inside under
the mosquito bar with various things from the
pack to put at the head of the bed under the
slant of the canvas. It smelled pleasantly of
canvas. Already there was something mysterious
and homelike. Nick was happy as he crawled
inside the tent. He had not been unhappy all
day. This was different though. Now things

were done. There had been this to do. Now it
was done. It had been a hard trip. He was
very tired. That was done. He had made his
camp. He was there, in the good place. He
was in his home where he had made it. Now he
was hungry. He came out, crawling under the
cheesecloth. It was quite dark outside. It
was lighter in the tent. Nick went over to
the pack and found, with his fingers, a long
nail in a paper sack of nails, in the bottom
of the pack. He drove it into the pine tree,
holding it close and hitting it gently with
the flat of the ax. He hung up the pack on the
nail. All his supplies were in the pack. They
were off the ground and sheltered now. Nick
was hungry. He did not believe he had ever
been hungrier. He opened and emptied a can of
pork and beans and a can of spaghetti into the
frying pan… He started a fire with some chunks
of pine he got from the stump. Over the fire
he stuck a wire grill, pushing the four legs
down into the ground with his boot. Nick put
the frying pan and a can of spaghetti on the
grill over the flames.'

*Ernest Hemingway – 'Big Two-Hearted River'
(1926).*

Hemingway's account may be picked apart. My drawing of Nick's camp is opposite. Nick's first decision was to find, recognise, decide upon the location for his place. He already had an idea in his mind of what he was going to do. And he had some ready-made components with him. He was going to make a place to sleep sheltered by a tent made with his sheet of canvas. The canvas would be supported by a rope. He needed two trees about the right distance apart between which he could stretch the rope. Before he started he knew what he wanted; he had an (architectural) idea ready. It was probably not one that he had generated himself; perhaps he had learnt it from seeing what others did. Still, it was he who decided to use this idea in this particular location. He had brought the requisite kit – canvas, rope, blankets, cheesecloth... with him.

He found two trees. An advantage was that they were on rising ground at the edge of the wood, with a view over the meadow, river and swamp. A refuge with a prospect is always a good place to be, neither out in the open nor completely hidden away, sparking neither agoraphobia nor claustrophobia, a location where you can see people coming and yet remain concealed. Although on a slope the ground between the trunks was level; it is not so comfortable to sleep on a slope.

It's not so comfortable either to sleep on lumpy roots, so Nick prepared the ground by removing the roots with his axe. Then he filled the holes and made the place even more comfortable with the layers of blankets. He changed the ground, making an area on which he could lie in relative comfort. The sleeping place was made. Most place-making (architecture) begins with changes to the ground surface. Nick's place also needed shelter from possible rain, so he stretched the rope between the trees to support the canvas which he pegged tight into the ground. He wanted to protect himself from mosquitoes too, so he hung his cheesecloth across the entrance. In these ways Nick responded to the conditions impinging on his place. Then he organised the inside putting the things he might need in the night at the head of his bed.

When all that was done Nick felt pleased. He was proud of the care he had taken in making his place. He enjoyed the psychological as well as physical comfort of the refuge he had made for himself. From the great outdoors he had created a small inside in which to hide himself to sleep. But he also needed a fire to cook his food. The hearth is an integral part of the architecture of Nick's camp. It would not have been sensible to put the fire inside the tent, but it is not clear from the description exactly where he did put it. We might guess that he would have placed it somewhere near, but not too near, the entrance to the tent. He would have been careful to clear away material that might catch and spread the fire. Maybe he made a circle of stones as a kerb. He had brought a grill to support his pan. He probably also found a log on which to sit while cooking. With the nail in the tree to hang his pack off the ground (not shown in my drawing), Nick's place was complete. It gave physical form to his existence in that location. It identified his place. It provided him with a temporary home, a centre to his life. While he was there it would frame, and act as a reference point for, everything he did. As its architect, Nick had not only provided himself with a comfortable place to sleep, he had made sense of the world around. (No wonder he felt happy!)

Exercise 12k. Framing atmospheres.

Try to make a place that contains a particular atmosphere.

Place-making is often associated with establishing, framing, encapsulating a change in atmosphere, either literally or metaphorically. The purpose of any simple shelter is to encapsulate a volume of space that will remain warm when the outside is cold or perhaps cool when the outside is hot, still when the outside is windy, dry when the outside is wet, private when the outside is public. These are the primary (practical) purposes of any home. An igloo, for example, encloses air warmed by the bodies of its occupants and perhaps also by a candle.

On the windy landscape of the Shetland Islands farmers build 'planty crubs'...

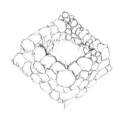

... which are small enclosures, defined by rough stone walls. They contain still air within which feed crops for animals will grow.

Travellers in the Gobi desert heat up stones in a fire and then mound earth over them to provide a bed in the open that will stay warm through the cold night.

But places (the places you make for the present exercise included) may frame different sorts of atmosphere too, and in different ways. Place-making can stimulate ingenuity. Nineteenth century anthropologists recorded Australian aborigine tribes building elaborate shaded platforms positioned over small fires so that they could rest out of the hot sun and with insects kept away by the smoke.

Some native North American tribes, as part of cleansing rituals, built sweat

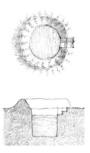

lodges (like Scandinavian saunas). Steam from water poured on hot stones would be trapped inside a simple shelter covered in animal skins (above).

Australian aborigines might make an 'igloo' out of twigs in which to isolate a young man preparing to go through an initiation ceremony.

If you are the person alone inside, in view of others outside, such a structure contains an unnerving atmosphere of isolation.

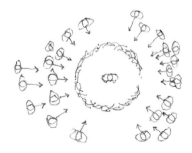

Places can frame the numinous too, they can contain an atmosphere felt to be sacred. At the beginning of Sophocles' tragedy *Oedipus at Colonus*, the self-blinded King Oedipus and his daughter Antigone reach Colonus within sight of the distant city of Athens. After their travels they seek to rest in a grove which they sense is sacred. Shortly they are warned by locals that they must not stay where they are because that spot is indeed dedicated to a god.

This drawing shows how the stage might be set for a performance of Sophocles' play. Even in this artificial environment, the place frames the sensed presence of the god; the god's spirit defines the place. Antigone and her father are framed within the halo of the place, isolated from the local people standing around.

191

As we have seen, nineteenth century anthropologists recorded people making totemic representations of animal gods...

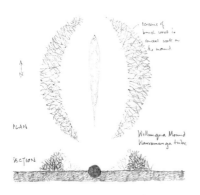

... and protecting them from sight by screens of brush, defining a place saturated with the spirit of the god. Most religions have done similar things. Churches not only shelter congregations during services, they enclose the sacred spirit of the religion. Even a small chapel in open countryside can contain and frame a sacred atmosphere.

Exercise 121. Setting down rules for using space.

Architecture sets the spatial matrix of our lives. Experiment with the ways in which you can manage the use of space by setting down 'rules' in the form of walls, doorways and other architectural elements.

Games pitches are clear examples.

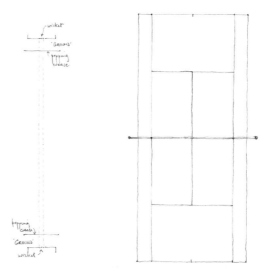

A cricket pitch and a tennis court are integral to the rule systems of their respective games. They consist of architectural elements: threshold; focus; wall. They set the spatial matrix within which their games are played.

It is similar with houses. A house sets the spatial matrix within which the

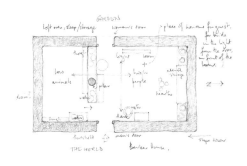

The space for a street magician's performance might be managed by a table and a rope laid on the pavement as a threshold to keep the audience at a distance.

life of its inhabitants is ordered. There are places for cooking, eating, sitting, watching television, working, growing plants...

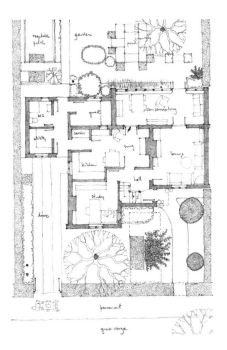

In his essay on 'The Berber House', the French anthropologist and philosopher Pierre Bourdieu described the spatial organisation of the houses of some north African people (top right). The house organised their lives, representing their social structures and spiritual beliefs.

The tents of desert tribes in Libya are organised to divide the realm of the women from that of the men. The realm of the

women is larger because that is where the work is done.

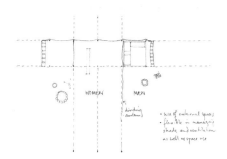

The space of these desert tents is managed by moveable fabric screens and tent roofs supported by posts and stretched by guy ropes.

Architecture sets the spatial matrix for rituals and ceremonies too. In his book *Black Elk Speaks*, John Neihardt recounts descriptions of the layout of ceremonial sites as told to him by an old Sioux chief. Rules determined how camps were to be set out, relating them to the wider world.

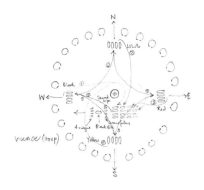

Such ceremonial sites contained within them detailed rules according to which the rituals should be performed. Intricate rituals were performed within a precise armature of markers indicating the cardinal directions from a centre to the great circle of the horizon.

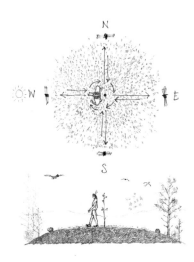

A warrior might have to perform ritual movements, perhaps walking from a central post, across a floor of flowers, towards each of the cardinal points in turn for a long period of time. In such circumstances the site becomes the framework for the choreography of the ritual.

In his film *Dogville* (2003), Lars von Trier alludes to the way architecture sets the rules of spatial interaction by representing the location of the story - a

tiny country town - as white lines on a black floor.

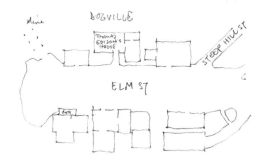

The lines on the black floor, like chalk lines on a black board, define the territories of the streets, houses and other buildings of the town. Like the lines of a games pitch, they set down the spatial rules within which the story is played out.

Even on the beach we organise our space, making places for parents and for children, in sun and shade, and with places for storing our belongings.

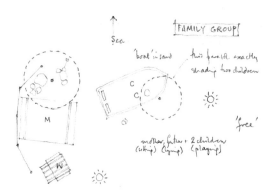

194

Exercise 12m. Experiment with time as an element of architecture.

Try making a sequence of places in the landscape that takes a person through a series of situations and experiences.

In these exercises you have already encountered time as an element of architecture. The doorway that some students made on the highest point of a sand dune is an example.

The doorway may be a static object identifying a particular stationary threshold at which the person sees the ocean or smells the forest, but it sets the focus for short series of experiences involving the element of time.

You can draw each of these series of experiences as (what film makers call) a storyboard. This is not only a way of recording experiences but a way of designing an orchestrated sequence of experiences too.

Your storyboard for the dune doorway might look like this. The sequence runs from top to bottom on the left hand side and then up the right. (There is no need for the drawings to be elaborate.)

1 spy the doorway

10 down to the forest

2 find the pathway

9 smell the trees

3 climb the dune

8 climb the dune

4 glimpse the sea

7 turn back

5 cross the threshold

6 down to the beach

195

You could extend this sequence, perhaps by providing a goal to reach after passing through the doorway. Maybe your goal is a marker on the beach...

... or a seat on which you can imagine yourself sitting like King Canute holding back the tide...

... or something unattainable.

Alternatively, your doorway might be the entrance into a labyrinth.

You might build a simple enclosure amongst the trees, hiding a space and generating a sense of mystery about what might be inside...

... with an obscure entrance that engenders a feeling of trepidation about entering the hidden world of the enclosure.

When you include time as an element of architecture it becomes like music or film, a medium through which you can elicit various emotions in the person. Orchestrating experience is a rich dimension of architecture.

IN YOUR NOTEBOOK...

In your notebook... draw the places you have made in the landscape.

You can draw your places as you see them with your eyes, as if you were taking a photograph of them. But it is more important that you draw them as they are in your mind, which is responsible for their form. As an architect, you must be able to see and understand all about the places you design and make, not just what they look like from the outside or from the inside. The most important drawings in designing and representing places are the plan and the section. These are the drawings of the mind not just the eyes; these are the drawings that illustrate the conceptual spatial organisation (the intellectual structure) of the work rather than just its visual appearance.

section

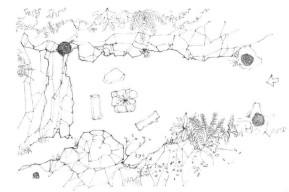

plan

The rocky clearing in the woods can be drawn as a plan and a section.

Draw your section above the plan to the same scale and facing in the appropriate direction so that the two drawings may be read together to conjure up a three dimensional understanding of the place in the mind of the person looking at the drawings. Try to be as accurate as possible about the size and positions of the most

197

significant elements of the place you are drawing. Other things (the branches and leaves of the trees for example) do not have to be accurate.

If you are drawing a place that you have made in a tree, then it is probably necessary to be more accurate about some of the most important branches.

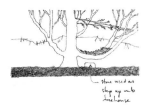

Show the construction of the elements you have built to define and frame your place.

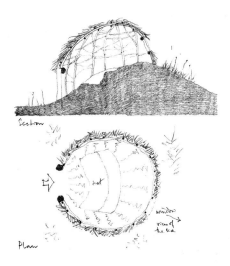

Show the construction in both section and plan. Again, be accurate about those things that need accuracy and sketchy about other things (such as the blades of grass). The ground is an essential element of all terrestrial architecture, so give all your sections a good portion of ground (shaded?) as a base for your construction. In plan you can indicate the slope of ground using shadows or wiggly lines as you wish. Some annotation can be useful, maybe to indicate the position of the sun or sea, or the direction of the wind.

As suggested on page 24 of *Analysing Architecture* (third edition, 2009) you will find a piece of squared paper, laid under your notebook paper, useful to help you control the position and scales of your drawings. It is also useful for keeping your notes neat and for shading in blocks of ground etc. Surprisingly the squared paper is useful in drawing irregular as well as regular places, and in drawing sections it reminds you constantly of the (rough) horizontality of the ground and the verticality of gravity. It helps you draw a straight and level horizon.

You should show what you can see in the background. Do not draw this background in perspective but at the same scale; hopefully you can see that this background is informative about the character of the space of the place you have made and its relationship with its surroundings.

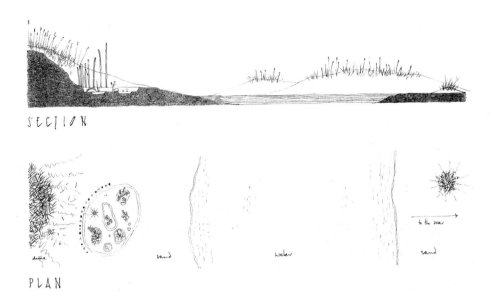

SECTION

PLAN

The context of your place is an essential ingredient of its identity (above). Although you know what the context is, that is not enough; you should also show it in your drawings, plans and especially sections. Be generous with the amount of context you show in your section. The context is an important part of the story of your place. In the woods the story of your place is likely to be constrained within quite a small area bounded by trees, but on the beach it is likely that your place will relate in some way to the ocean and the distant horizon. Your drawings should communicate this relationship. You might wish to draw your section at two different scales - one that shows the detail of your place close to, and one that shows the relationship of your place with the wider landscape.

Through practice you should strive to achieve a state of mind where you really enjoy the experience of drawing, the sensuality of making marks with, for example, a pencil on a piece of paper; you should be discriminating about which sort of pencil, which lead, which paper... is right for you and what you are doing; you should relish the time spent shading a tone evenly, or drawing a tree.

If the main idea of your place is to do with a relationship with the horizon, then do a drawing that illustrates that idea (in a way more powerful than could be done with words).

199

IN YOUR NOTEBOOK...

In your notebook... find and draw examples of buildings that exploit or mitigate the conditions within which they are set.

Most buildings relate actively to their conditions in one way or another. Your task in your notebook is to understand how, and to note down, using drawings, the ways in which they do so.

Castles and fortresses for example exploit high ground to obtain a panoramic view of the surrounding countryside, to watch out for attackers, and to establish a visible presence for authority.

Like a non-authoritarian fortress, Condominium One at Sea Ranch (Moore, Lyndon, Turnbull, Whitaker, 1965, one of the Case Studies in *Twenty Buildings*) also relates to dramatic conditions. It is set on the rugged and windswept North California coast. Its site is protected from incessant winds by large hedgerows, but the building itself forms a protective courtyard whilst also allowing each dwelling a view of the crashing ocean and blinding sunsets.

Analyse how your own house responds to its conditions. Find further examples in journals and books too. Learn about how architecture mediates between the person and the world around.

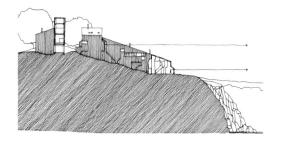

SUMMARY OF SECTION THREE

Architecture is of the mind and also of
the world. It depends on ideas. But ideas
are modified by what happens to them in
reality. In the first two sections of this
book, the exercises took place mainly in a
special isolated realm – your bread board –
an arena (*chora*) which was a manifestation
of the space of your mind. In this realm
you built models from children's building
blocks of rectangular geometry and standard
dimensions. This was a playground of your
imagination. From the real world, only
gravity, light and the scaled size of a
model (inanimate and ideal) person entered
your playground. If you had confined
yourself to drawing, on paper or computer,
even these need not have impinged on the
architectural games of your mind.

In this last section, the exercises have
invited you to take your mind out into the
real world and asked it to apply its ideas
to real materials, in real conditions, with
real people. In doing so the exercises have
prompted you to realise that places may be
identified by choice and recognition, they
can be established merely by occupation
without amendment. Architecture can be a
matter of modifying found places.

Modifying the world to accommodate
life, possessions, activities... involves
exploiting available resources (materials,
skills, topography, sunshine, breezes...),
responding to human needs, and countering
threats (cold winds, wet rain, predatory

animals, human enemies...). Architecture
also involves being sensitive to the
inherent characteristics of materials
available, being aware of the ways in which
they have their own geometries of making,
and capacities for supporting themselves
and other elements.

But architecture is more than pragmatic.
It frames atmospheres. As non-verbal
philosophy, it can set down spatial rules
or guidelines for making sense of the
world. Like film, music, narrative... it
can orchestrate experience and elicit
changing emotions.

In any art, quality comes with
progressive revision and refinement.
Reflect on what you have done. Revise it.
Take the opportunity, if you can, to take
your own assessment and the assessments of
others into account, and make your places
better (in whatever terms emerge from the
assessment, or in any other way). You are
already on the road to being a professional
architect, committed (dedicated) to
informing the world and making it better
(more beautiful, more interesting, more
comfortable, better organised...) by
application of its most powerful tool
- your informed imagination - and the
realisation of ideas in physical form.

POSTLUDE: Drawing plans and sections

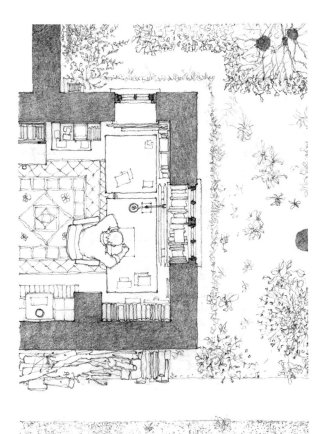

Architecture should be depicted not just as it appears to the eye but as it appears to the mind.

In his book My Name is Red *(1998, page 90), the writer Orhan Pamuk describes traditional miniature paintings:*

'You know those palace, hamam and castle pictures that were made in Tabriz and Shiraz for a time; so that the picture might replicate the piercing gaze of Exalted Allah, who sees and understands all, the miniaturist would depict the palace in cross-section as though having cut it in half with a huge, magical straight razor, and he'd paint all the interior details – which could otherwise never be seen from outside – down to the pots and pans, drinking glasses, wall ornamentation, curtains, caged parrots, the most private corners, and the pillows on which reclined a lovely maiden such as had never seen the light of day.'

You could draw a picture of the outside of your house or of a room inside. But if you draw a section and a plan you can show the inside and the outside at the same time. You can show how they relate to each other through windows and doorways, under trees and over hedges.

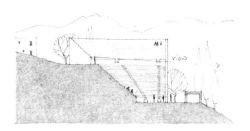

Often places in the landscape have important relationships with their wider context. Your drawings, especially the section, should show this. In the case of the Greek theatre at Segesta on the island of Sicily you might draw a section through a wide tract of landscape to illustrate the relationship between the theatre and the surrounding mountains. The actual theatre might be quite small in such a drawing but you can do another section at a larger scale to show its form.

The seat under the tree in the drawing on the left is a pleasant place to sit but you would not be telling its full story - its position on the cliff top with views across the sea but in contact with the town... - if you did not draw a generous section. You must be the judge of how much to show in order to tell the relevant story of your place fully.

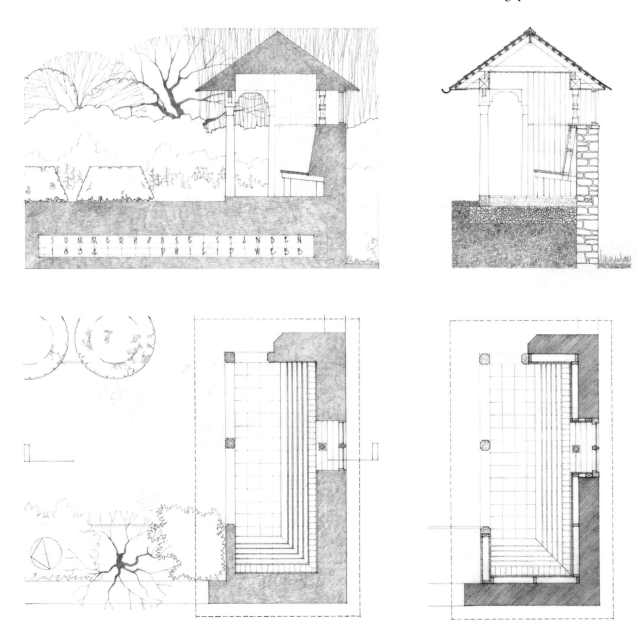

There are two main kinds of plan and section drawings: 'construction' drawings (right) and 'design' drawings (left). In 'construction' drawings your intention is to show how your building is made, so you show the different materials and the ways in which they come together. In 'design' drawings your intention is to show the space of your place, what it accommodates and its relationship with its context, so you show none of the cross-sectional constructional detail; you show all the solid material that the section cuts through – building and ground – in the same way with no joins.

These drawings are of a small summer house designed in the late nineteenth century for the gardens of Standen in Sussex by the architect Philip Webb. Measuring buildings and drawing them – as 'design' and as 'construction' plans and sections (you will have to make some educated guesses about hidden construction) – is a good way to practice your drawing and develop your understanding of architecture, how it works and what you can do with it. You can do this in any medium – pencil, pen, or on a computer... – to study any building. If you do not have opportunity to measure, you can do it from published sources.

ACKNOWLEDGEMENTS

Sincere thanks to:

John Bush, University of Huddersfield, for pointing me in the direction of Peter Brook and his ideas on informal theatre spaces in the book *The Open Circle*.

Tom Killian, New York, for sending me the description of Nick's camp from Ernest Hemingway's 'Big Two-Hearted River'.

Jeff Balmer, University of North Carolina Charlotte, for inviting me to the Beginning Design Education conference held at his university in 2010; and Michael T. Swisher, at the same university, for sharing his ideas on First Year architectural education.

Lisa Landrum, University of Manitoba Winnipeg, for pointing me to the Greek verb 'to architect'.

Matthew Brehm, University of Idaho, for expressing interest in my notebooks.

Robert Atkinson at Richmond upon Thames College, London, for showing me the work of his students studying for an 'A' level in architecture.

Alan Paddison for reporting on the dolmen of *La Bajoulière* in the Loire region of France.

Fran Ford, Laura Williamson and Alanna Donaldson at Routledge for their support through the project.

And, last but by no means least, to those generations of students who have put up with, and often enthusiastically engaged in, the various exercises I have set them (for example in the wind and rain of Welsh and Scottish beaches).

READING

Fundamentals

Gille Deleuze and Félix Guattari, translated by Massumi – '1837: Of the Refrain', in *A Thousand Plateaus: Capitalism and Schizophrenia* (1980), Continuum, New York, 1987.

Aldo van Eyck – 'Labyrinthian Clarity', in Donat (editor) – *World Architecture 3*, Studio Vista, London, 1966.

Aldo van Eyck – 'Place and Occasion' (1962), in Hertzberger and others – *Aldo van Eyck*, Stichting Wonen, Amsterdam, 1982.

Martin Heidegger, translated by Hofstader – 'Building Dwelling Thinking' and '… poetically man dwells…', in *Poetry, Language and Thought* (1971), Harper and Row, London and New York, 1975.

Dom H. van der Laan, translated by Padovan – *Architectonic Space: Fifteen Lessons on the Disposition of the Human Habitat*, E.J. Brill, Leiden, 1983.

Charles Moore and others – *The Place of Houses*, Holt Rinehart and Winston, New York, 1974.

Christian Norberg-Schulz – *Existence, Space and Architecture*, Studio Vista, London, 1971.

Steen Eiler Rasmussen – *Experiencing Architecture*, MIT Press, Cambridge, Mass., 1959.

August Schmarsow, translated by Mallgrave and Ikonomou – 'The Essence of Architectural Creation' (1893), in Mallgrave and Ikonomou (editors) - *Empathy, Form, and Space*, The Getty Center for the History of Art and the Humanities, Santa Monica, Calif., 1994.

Simon Unwin – *Doorway*, Routledge, Abingdon, 2007.

Geometry

Werner Blaser – *The Rock is My Home*, WEMA, Zurich, 1976.

James W. P. Campbell and Will Pryce – *Brick: A World History*, Thames and Hudson, London, 2003.

Le Corbusier, translated by de Francia and Bostock – *The Modulor, a Harmonious Measure to the Human Scale Universally Applicable to Architecture and Mechanics*, Faber and Faber, London, 1961.

John Dee – *Mathematicall Praeface to the Elements of Geometrie of Euclid of Megara* (1570), facsimile edition, Kessinger Publishing, Whitefish, MT., undated.

Tore Drange, Hans Olaf Aanensen and Jon Brænne – *Gamle Trehus*, Universitetsforlaget, Oslo, 1980.

Peter Eisenman – *The Formal Basis of Modern Architecture*, Lars Müller Publishers, Switzerland, 2006.

Suzanne Frank – *Peter Eisenman's House VI: the Client's Response*, Whitney Library of Design, New York, 1994.

Eileen Gray and Jean Badovici – 'De l'éclecticism au doute' ('From eclecticism to doubt'), in *L'Architecture Vivante*, Winter 1929, p. 19.

Eileen Gray and Jean Badovici – 'Description' (of Villa E.1027), in *L'Architecture Vivante*, Winter 1929, p. 3.

Herb Greene – *Mind and Image*, Granada, London, 1976.

Cecil Hewett – *English Cathedral and Monastic Carpentry*, Phillimore, Chichester, 1985.

Nathaniel Lloyd – *A History of English Brickwork: with examples and notes of the architectural use and manipulation of brick from mediaeval times to the end of the Georgian period* (1925), Antique Collectors' Club Ltd, London, 1999.

Richard Padovan – *Proportion: Science, Philosophy, Architecture*, E. & F.N. Spon, London, 1999.

Colin Rowe – 'The Mathematics of the Ideal Villa' (1947), in *The Mathematics of the Ideal Villa and Other Essays*, MIT Press, Cambridge, Mass., 1976.

Bernard Rudofsky – *Architecture Without Architects*, Academy Editions, London, 1964.

Bernard Rudofsky – *The Prodigious Builders*, Secker and Warburg, London, 1977.

Alison Smithson – 'Beatrix Potter's Places', in *Architectural Design*, Volume 37, December 1967, p. 573.

Alison Smithson, editor – *Team 10 Primer*, MIT Press, Cambridge, Mass., 1968.

Arturo Tedeschi – *Parametric architecture with Grasshopper*, Le Penseur, Italy, 2011.

Rudolf Wittkower – *Architectural Principles in the Age of Humanism*, Tiranti, London, 1952.

Lim Jee Yuan – *The Malay House*, Institut Masyarakat, Malaysia, 1987.

Out into the real world

Jay Appleton – *The Experience of Landscape* (1975), Hull University Press/ John Wiley, London, 1986.

Pierre Bourdieu – 'The Berber House', translated in Mary Douglas, editor – *Rules and Meanings*, Penguin, London, 1973, pp. 98-110.

Peter Brook – *The Empty Space*, Penguin, London, 2008.

Antonio Damasio – *The Feeling of What Happens: Body, Emotion and the Making of Consciousness*, Vintage, London, 2000.

Glyn E. Daniel – *Megaliths in History*, Thames and Hudson, London, 1972.

Glyn E. Daniel – *The Prehistoric Chamber Tombs of England and Wales*, Cambridge UP, 1950.

Andrea Deplazes, editor – *Constructing Architecture: Materials, Processes, Structures*, Birkhäuser, Basel, 2005.

I.E.S. Edwards – *The Pyramids of Egypt*, Penguin, London, 1971.

Mircea Eliade, translated by Sheed – 'Sacred Places: Temple, Palace, "Centre of the World" ', chapter in *Patterns in Comparative Religion*, Sheed and Ward, London, 1958.

Mircea Eliade, translated by Trask – 'Sacred Space and Making the World Sacred', chapter in *The Sacred and the Profane: the Nature of Religion*, Harcourt Brace and Company, London, 1958.

Sverre Fehn, edited by Marja-Riitta Norri and Marja Kärkkäinen – *Sverre Fehn: the Poetry of the Straight Line*, Museum of Finnish Architecture, Helsinki, 1992.

Vittorio Gregotti – 'Address to the Architectural League, New York, October 1982', in *Section A*, Volume 1, Number 1, Feb/Mar 1983, p. 8.

Lawrence Halprin – *The Sea Ranch... Diary of an Idea*, Spacemaker Press, Berkeley CA, 2002.

Roger Joussaume, translated by Chippindale – *Dolmens for the Dead: Megalith Building Throughout the World* (1985), Guild Publishing, London, 1988.

Susan Kent, editor – *Domestic Architecture and the Use of Space*, Cambridge University Press, Cambridge, 1990.

R.D. Martienssen – *The Idea of Space in Greek Architecture*, Witwatersrand UP, Johannesburg, 1968.

Ray Mears – *Bushcraft*, Coronet Books, Philadelphia, PA, 2004.

John G. Neihardt – *Black Elk Speaks* (1932), University of Nebraska Press, 1979.

Kevin Nute – *Place, Time and Being in Japanese Architecture*, Routledge, London, 2004.

Amos Rapoport – *House Form and Culture*, Prentice Hall, New Jersey, 1969.

Edward Relph – *Place and Placelessness*, Pion, London, 1976.

Vincent Scully – *The Earth, the Temple, and the Gods; Greek Sacred Architecture*, Yale UP, New Haven and London, 1962.

Gottfried Semper, translated by Mallgrave and Hermann – *The Four Elements of Architecture* (1851), MIT Press, Cambridge MA., 1989.

Baldwin Spencer and F.J. Gillen – *The Native Tribes of Central Australia*, Macmillan, London, 1899.

Henry David Thoreau – *Walden* (1854), Bantam, New York, 1981.

Andrew Todd and Jean-Guy Lecat – *The Open Circle*, Palgrave Macmillan, New York, 2003.

Simon Unwin – 'Architecture as Identification of Place', in *Analysing Architecture*, Routledge, Abingdon, 2009.

Simon Unwin – 'Constructing Place on the Beach', in Menin, editor – *Constructing Place: Mind and Matter*, Routledge, Abingdon, 2003.

Colin St John Wilson – 'Masters of Building: Sigurd Lewerentz', in *Architects Journal*, 13 April, 1988, pp. 31-52.

Colin St John Wilson – 'Sigurd Lewerentz: the Sacred Buildings and the Sacred Sites', in *Architectural Reflections: Studies in the Philosophy and Practice of Architecture* (1992), Manchester UP, 2000, pp. 110-137.

Peter Zumthor – *Thinking Architecture*, Birkhäuser, Basel, 1998.

Peter Zumthor – *Atmospheres*, Birkhäuser, Basel, 2006.

Drawing

Francis D. Ching – *Architectural Graphics*, John Wiley and Son, New York, 2007.

Francis D. Ching – *Architecture: Form, Space and Order*, John Wiley and Son, New York, 2007.

Robert Chitham – *Measured Drawing for Architects*, Architectural Press, London, 1980.

Norman Crowe and Paul Laseau – *Visual Notes for Architects and Designers*, John Wiley and Son, 1986.

Lorraine Farrelly – *Basics Architecture: Representational Techniques*, AVA Publishing, Worthing, 2007.

Paul Laseau – *Freehand Sketching: an Introduction*, W.W. Norton, London, 2004.

Edward Robbins – *Why Architects Draw*, MIT Press, Cambridge, MA, 1994.

Simon Unwin – 'Notebook Architecture', in Wendy Gunn, editor – *Fieldnotes and Sketchbooks*, Peter Lang, Frankfurt, 2009

Lawrence Weschler – *Seeing is Forgetting the Name of the Thing One Sees: a Life of Contemporary Artist Robert Irwin*, University of California Press, Berkeley, 1982.

INDEX